TOM DOYLE

THE
INCREDIBLE
JOURNEY

A Concise Road Map from Genesis to Revelation

UNCHARTED
PRESS

Copyright © 2022 by Thomas J. Doyle
ISBN: 979-8-218-00368-5

All rights reserved. No part of this publication may be reproduced, distributed, or transmitted in any form or by any means, including photocopying, recording, or other electronic or mechanical methods, without the prior written permission of the publisher, except in the case of brief quotations embodied in critical reviews and certain other noncommercial uses permitted by copyright law. For permission requests, write or email the publisher per the contact information below:

Uncharted Press
2001 W. Plano Parkway
Plano, Texas 75075
info@unchartedministries.com
www.unchartedministries.com

Unless otherwise indicated, Scripture quotations are taken from the Holy Bible, New International Version®, NIV® Copyright ©1973, 1978, 1984, 2011 by Biblica, Inc.® Used by permission. All rights reserved worldwide.

Scripture quotations marked RSV are taken from the Revised Standard Version of the Bible, copyright © 1946, 1952, and 1971 the Division of Christian Education of the National Council of the Churches of Christ in the United States of America. Used by permission. All rights reserved.

Produced in association with New Vantage Publishing Partners and the DRS Agency, Franklin, Tennessee.

Agenting • Publishing • Marketing

www.drsagency.com

Contents

Introduction	

Old Testament

Genesis	10
Exodus	18
Leviticus	22
Numbers	25
Deuteronomy	28
Joshua	30
Judges	33
Ruth	37
1 Samuel	40
2 Samuel	44
1 Kings	47
2 Kings	50
1 and 2 Chronicles	53
Ezra	57
Nehemiah	60
Esther	64
Job	67
Psalms	71
Proverbs	75
Ecclesiastes	78
Song of Solomon	80
Isaiah	82
Jeremiah	87
Lamentations	90
Ezekiel	92
Daniel	95
Hosea	98
Joel	100
Amos	102
Obadiah	104
Jonah	106
Micah	108
Nahum	110
Habakkuk	113
Zephaniah	115
Haggai	117
Zechariah	119
Malachi	121

New Testament

Matthew	124
Mark	128
Luke	131
John	133
Acts	136
Romans	139
1 Corinthians	142
2 Corinthians	144
Galatians	146
Ephesians	148
Philippians	150
Colossians	152
1 Thessalonians	154
2 Thessalonians	156
1 Timothy	157
2 Timothy	159
Titus	161
Philemon	163
Hebrews	164
James	166
1 Peter	168
2 Peter	170
1 John	172
2 John	174
3 John	175
Jude	176
Revelation	177

Charts

Judges	34
Joshua and Judges	36
1 Samuel	42
1 and 2 Kings	51
Elijah and Elisha	52
Samuel, Kings, and Chronicles	55
Nehemiah	62
Historical and Poetical Books	67
Daniel	97
Isaiah and Micah	108
Zechariah's Visions	120
Between the Testaments	122

Additional Resources

Israel Timeline	184
Israel's and Judah's Kings	186
God's Concern for the Nations	187
Prophecies	189
Notes	*190*

Introduction

The Apostle and the Traveler

Your word is a lamp for my feet, a light on my path.
—Psalm 119:105

Life is filled with journeys. The most important one we take is the journey with God throughout our days on the earth. At the center of our relationship with our Father is the Bible. God revealed Himself to us with an up-close-and-personal picture on every page of Scripture. We can know what His character is like and we can know Him intimately by just opening this amazing book. The Bible was not written to merely give us information. It was written to transform our lives. But this will never happen if we don't understand it.

In the book of Acts, the apostle Philip encountered a man who was on a journey himself. While on the road, the traveler was reading from the prophet Isaiah, and Philip asked him this profound question: "Do you understand what you are reading?" The man from Ethiopia answered: "How can I unless someone explains it to me?" (8:30–31).

The interchange between the apostle and the traveler explains precisely why *The Incredible Journey* was written. The Bible is a large book, and it also can be confusing at times. It requires explanation. Surely God didn't write it and hope that somehow we might get a clue along the way as to what it means. He wants us to study the Scriptures, understand them, and then live them. But we must be trained how.

The Incredible Journey is a short Bible survey that will help you navigate your way through the Bible from cover to cover. Each book is summarized and explained so you can maximize your daily Bible reading and aim at living out the truths contained in each one. Reading through the Bible is one of the most important things we can do, and we pray that this resource serves to guide you all along the way.

Have an Incredible Journey!

Tom Doyle

The Word of God
The Book that Changes Lives

"Give me a Bible and a candle and shut me up in a dungeon, and I will tell you what the world is doing." —*an old divine saying*

"[The] New Testament . . . is the best book that ever was, or will be, known in the world."[1] —*Charles Dickens*

"Let the world progress as much as it likes, let all branches of human research develop to the very utmost, nothing will take the place of the Bible."[2] —*Johann Wolfgang von Goethe*

"It is impossible mentally and socially to enslave a Bible-reading people. The principles of the Bible are the ground-work of human freedom."[3] —*Horace Greeley*

"[The Bible] is a book worth more than all the other books that were ever printed."[4] —*Patrick Henry*

"There is one thing more I wish I could leave you all—the religion of Jesus Christ. With this, though you had nothing else, you could be happy; without this, though you had all things else, you could not be happy."[5] —*Patrick Henry's will*

"The best evidence of the Bible being the word of God is to be found between its covers."[6] —*Charles Hodge*

"The study of this Book in your Bible classes is a postgraduate course in the richest library of human experience."[7] —*Herbert Hoover*

"If a man's Bible is coming apart, it is an indication that he himself is fairly well put together."[8] —*James E. Jennings*

"[The Bible] is the best gift God has given to man. All the good the Saviour gave to the world was communicated through this book."[9] —*Abraham Lincoln*

"This Book will keep you from sin, or sin will keep you from this Book."[10] —*Dwight L. Moody*

INTRODUCTION

The Nature of the Bible

The Eight Wonders of the Bible—God's Masterpiece

1. The Wonder of Its Construction
God put it together over a period of 1,500 years.

2. The Wonder of Its Unity
God used forty different authors to write sixty-six books, yet it remains completely unified and consistent.

3. The Wonder of Its Historical Accuracy
The Bible has never been proved wrong.

4. The Wonder of Its Scientific Accuracy
Although not a book of science, when the Bible speaks on the subject, it is scientifically accurate.

5. The Wonder of Its Indestructibility
Though attempted repeatedly, the Bible can never be destroyed completely—by man or government.

6. The Wonder of Its Prophecy
The Bible has the ability to predict the future with 100 percent accuracy.

7. The Wonder of Its Christ-Centeredness
From cover to cover, the Bible presents Christ as the center of the Scriptures.

8. The Wonder of Its Transforming Capabilities
Since the Bible is alive, it has the ability to transform us inwardly.

Conclusion:
The Bible is the most amazing book ever written. God wrote it through human authors over several centuries, yet it remains cohesive and consistent in theme from Genesis to Revelation. It is a divinely written miraculous book that produces growth in believers and brings light to the world. It is the power of God that produced it, protects it, and propagates it around the world to be the true Bread of Life for all.

OLD TESTAMENT

Genesis
The Book of Beginnings

OUTLINE
1. Event 1: Creation (1)
2. Event 2: Fall (3:1–7)
3. Event 3: Flood (6–9)
4. Event 4: Babel (11:1–9)
5. Great Men 1: Abraham (12:1–3)
6. Great Men 2: Isaac (18:9–14)
7. Great Men 3: Jacob (25:21–26)
8. Great Men 4: Joseph (37–50)

INTRODUCTION

Genesis is in many ways the most important book in the Bible. In this pivotal book we learn who God is, how man failed, and how Satan tempts us to sin. God provides the solution to our sins in the descendant of Abraham, who would bless the whole world. His name would be Jesus.

FAST FACTS
- Genesis was written by Moses in approximately 1450 BC.
- Genesis through Deuteronomy is called the Law or Pentateuch—which means "five books." The books were authored by Moses.
- Genesis 1:1: "In the beginning" is to be understood as not the beginning of eternity but of the creation of the world.
- The first verse of the Bible is the watershed verse on which everything else hinges. Why?
  - If you can handle this, you can handle all other biblical miracles.
  - God refutes all false belief systems—atheism, agnosticism, and other false religions—in this first verse of the Bible.
  - It asserts that God was preexistent—man did not invent God.

IMPORTANT WORD STUDY
- **"Created"**: *Bara* in Hebrew always means to make something out of nothing. This term is only used in Scripture with reference to God. We can't create—we can't even think of something that isn't just a part of something else. *Bara* is used in the first verse of the Bible.
- **"Creation,"** therefore, is "ex nihilo," or literally "from nothing." A New Testament verse that describes this is Hebrews 11:3.

HERBERT SPENCER
In the nineteenth century, English philosopher Herbert Spencer was nominated for the Nobel Prize for Literature for his discovery that all natural phenomena are "manifestations" either "vivid" or "faint," and are then segregated further into the following five categories:[11]
1. Time
2. Force
3. Motion (or, Action)
4. Space
5. Matter

Spencer was hailed as a genius, yet he never realized that God had already revealed this to man in the very first verse of the Bible!
1. Time: "In the beginning"
2. Force: "God"
3. Action: "created"
4. Space: "heavens"
5. Matter: "earth"

In Genesis we see three starts for mankind, beginning with a central figure in each start:
1. Adam
2. Noah
3. Abraham

Each figure is pivotal in the overall plan for mankind, and each represents one-third of the puzzle for all of human history. It is divided this way:

1. Adam: fell to the power of sin
2. Noah: the judgment of sin
3. Abraham: redemption from sin

EVENT 1: CREATION—GENESIS 1

The Bible teaches that God is eternal. He always was. God created all living things during Creation. God saved the best for last in His Creation. King David would write about this several centuries later: *"When I consider your heavens, the work of your fingers, the moon and the stars, which you have set in place, what is mankind that you are mindful of them, human beings that you care for them? You have made them a little lower than the angels and crowned them with glory and honor"* (Psalm 8:3–5). Mankind is, as David demonstrated, "the crown of Creation."

Here is the order in which God made everything:
Day 1 Light
Day 2 Sky and water
Day 3 Land, the seas, and vegetation
Day 4 Sun, moon, stars, days, months, seasons
Day 5 Fish and birds
Day 6 Animals, man, and woman
Day 7 God rested and declared that creation was good

In the garden of Eden, God performed the first marriage between Adam and Eve. Man was incomplete without woman. Marriage was God's idea, and He Himself gave it as a gift to humanity. The husband-wife relationship that produces children and is called family is the basis for all societies.

Question: Does "day" refer to a twenty-four-hour period or a geological period that could be thousands of years?

Answer: The Hebrew word used in the Creation account, *yom*, is a literal day used all through the Old Testament (e.g., Exodus 20:11). Therefore, it makes sense to see creation in terms of literal twenty-four-hour days, rather than geological periods.

There are great implications from creation: Everything that exists is under God's control, including nature, enemies, creatures, and all inventions.

1. **Basis of Law**: If God is before all things and made all things, how foolish it is to have any other gods before Him. There are none!
2. **His Character**: God's plan involves bringing darkness to light.
    a. 2 Corinthians 4:6: *"Let light shine out of darkness."*
    b. 1 John 1:5: *"God is light; in him there is no darkness at all."*

EVENT 2: FALL—GENESIS 3:1-7
REASON FOR THE FALL:
God's commands were not followed. The plunge into sin was progressive:
- Genesis 3:1: Doubt—Satan challenged everything God said and tried to place doubt in Adam's and Eve's hearts.
- Genesis 3:2-3: Misunderstanding the word—Eve was not clear on what God had actually said concerning the tree.
- Genesis 3:4-5: Unbelief—Satan again challenged God's authority with a lie, and Eve believed it. We disobey God because we do not believe He will follow through on what He says.

RESULTS OF THE FALL:
Sin permeated the human race through this one act. Romans 5:12 says, "Therefore, just as sin entered the world through one man, and death through sin, . . . in this way death came to all men, because all sinned." Satan won this battle. Jesus showed in the New Testament that Satan could be defeated easily. How can we ensure victory against Satan?

The answer is found in Matthew 4:1-11, where Jesus is confronted by Satan. Three times Jesus said, *"It is written."* Jesus continually used the authority of God's Word. Satan cannot defeat it since it is based on God's power and authority.

EVENT 3: FLOOD—GENESIS 6-9
After only five chapters in the Bible, sin is so widespread that God must start over. In perhaps one of the saddest verses in all of Scripture, God reveals His feelings about the devastating effect sin has had on the human race.

Genesis 6:5–7: *"The LORD saw how great the wickedness of the human race had become on the earth, and that every inclination of the thoughts of the human heart was only evil all the time. The LORD regretted that he had made human beings on the earth, and his heart was deeply troubled. So the LORD said, 'I will wipe from the face of the earth the human race I have created—and with them the animals, the birds and the creatures that move along the ground—for I regret that I have made them.'"*

God found a man with whom to start the human race over. Despite sin infesting the entire world, one man rose above it and followed God. Noah was found righteous, and God selected him to build humanity again. Noah's formula for remaining pure amid the evil was simple yet effective: *"Noah was a righteous man, blameless among the people of his time, and he walked faithfully with God"* (Genesis 6:9).

The Flood was a universal deluge of water that covered the globe. Since *"all the high mountains under the entire heavens were covered"* (Genesis 7:19), a localized flood is ruled out. Three other points of evidence for a worldwide flood are contained in the text:
1. God said He would put an end to "all" people. (Genesis 6:13)
2. Water covered "all the surface of the earth" for one year. (Genesis 8:9, 13)
3. The rainbow was a covenant promise from God to "all" mankind. (Genesis 9:8–17)

EVENT 4: BABEL—GENESIS 11:1–9
The first command God gave after the Flood is found in Genesis 9:1–2:
"Then God blessed Noah and his sons, saying to them, 'Be fruitful and increase in number and fill the earth. The fear and dread of you will fall on all the beasts of the earth, and on all the birds in the sky, on every creature that moves along the ground, and on all the fish in the sea; they are given into your hands.'"

The people of the day started the disobedience cycle again by rejecting God. The Tower of Babel was a symbol of defiance. In present-day Iraq, ziggurats (towers that spiral upward) have been found from the time period of the

Tower of Babel. On top of these ziggurats, zodiac signs have been found, indicating star worship.

THE RESULTS OF THE TOWER OF BABEL

All nations and all people groups began here. The divisive results of the Tower of Babel are seen in the more than two hundred nations present in today's world. Many of these countries have multiple cultures and multiple dialects within them. The tiny country of Papua New Guinea alone has more than eight hundred languages.[12] Your cultural heritage and language make you distinct from the others. One day all of this will change. God will take all the nations full circle and bring them back together again. Revelation 7:9 shows that the nations of the world will finally be reunited again. It foretells a time when people of every nation, tribe, and language will have representatives worshipping God and the Lamb of God.

GREAT MEN 1: ABRAHAM—GENESIS 12:1-3

Immediately after the Tower of Babel, God selected a nation to be His light among the nations. Abraham would be the father of that nation, called Israel. God's promise to Abraham contains five "I wills":
1. I will make you into a great nation.
2. I will bless you.
3. I will make your name great, and you will be a blessing.
4. I will bless those who bless you.
5. I will curse [those who curse you].

Abraham is the father of our faith. God's unconditional promise to bless the descendants of Abraham is based on the integrity of God and not the ability of man. Therefore, the conditions of the covenant are still in effect to this day. Today, God blesses those who bless Israel. He also curses those who curse Israel. The descendant of Abraham that would bless the world was Jesus. Matthew 1:1-2, says *"This is the genealogy of Jesus the Messiah the son of David, the son of Abraham: Abraham was the father of Isaac, Isaac the father of Jacob, Jacob the father of Judah and his brothers . . ."* Abraham was middle-aged, prosperous, and settled. His roots were pagan, yet he left everything and followed the call of God, even though God did not tell him where He was taking him.

GREAT MEN 2: ISAAC—GENESIS 18:9-14

Why is Isaac important? Because his birth shows that God keeps *all* of His promises. God can bypass nature at any time to accomplish His purposes. Sarah was ninety years old, and God allowed her to conceive. Abraham's descendants validate God's purposes. Isaac was the miracle child born to a couple past the age of reproduction. In a supreme test of faith, Abraham was commanded by God to sacrifice Isaac on an altar. Abraham willingly took Isaac to the point of death, and then God intervened to stop the sacrifice. Two things were significant about the event:
- Abraham was obedient even though it would cost him his son's life.
- The place he was to sacrifice his son was called Mount Moriah. This mountain would be the future place of Israel's temples. Thousands of animals would be sacrificed here, culminating with God's sacrifice of His own Son, Jesus, on Mount Moriah.

GREAT MEN 3: JACOB—GENESIS 25:21-26

Jacob's name was changed to "Israel" which means "he strives with God." Though he was characteristically "sneaky," as his name implies in Hebrew, God used him anyway. Jacob received his brother, Esau's, birthright. This is borne out in history, as Israel is God's inheritance, and Edomite descendants from Esau were finally wiped out by God. God's promises to Abraham are continued through Jacob, and God renamed him accordingly.

GREAT MEN 4: JOSEPH—GENESIS 37-50

Joseph was the favorite of Jacob's twelve sons. Out of jealousy, Joseph's brothers kidnapped him and sold him into slavery. Joseph ended up in Egypt, and God used him to spare the family of Israel during a massive famine. Because of his strong character in the midst of adversity, he rose from slave to the second most powerful man in Egypt. Only God could accomplish this.

Joseph is an Old Testament picture of Christ:
- Always faithful
- Used by God to do the miraculous

- Charged, yet not guilty
- Shown committing no sin

Genesis ends with the promises to Abraham unfulfilled. The descendants of Abraham are in Egypt, and the land guaranteed to them is yet to be taken.

Exodus
The Book of Israel's Beginning

OUTLINE
1. Israel in Egypt (1–13)
2. From Egypt to Sinai (14–19)
3. The Giving of the Law (20–24)
4. The Tabernacle (25–40)

INTRODUCTION

Exodus is, in a very real sense, a continued story. The first word in the Hebrew text is the conjunction *And*. At the close of Genesis we see the chosen family in Egypt, and Joseph occupying a great place of power. The time gap between Genesis 50 and Exodus 1 is approximately four hundred years.

FAST FACTS
- The author is Moses.
- Exodus means "departure." It was written about 1450 BC.
- The theme is redemption.
- The significance of Exodus is threefold.
  - Israel becomes a nation. Genesis presents Israel as a family. In Exodus they number about 2.5 million.
  - Redemption is explained. The Red Sea miracle is the Old Testament picture of salvation.
  - With redemption comes responsibility. The law is given to the new nation.

TOPIC 1: ISRAEL IN EGYPT—EXODUS 1–13

The family of Jacob became the nation of Israel. Genesis 46:27 tells us that Jacob's family relocated to Egypt and numbered 70 people in all. In Numbers 1, we are told that there were 603,000 males. Normally, males made up one-fourth of the population. To achieve this population in four hundred years, an annual growth rate would be about 10 percent. Thus in one hundred years, Israel went from a population of 70 to about 2.5 million. How could Israel achieve this? Only through God's help. Exodus 1:20 says that *"God was kind . . . and the people increased and became even more numerous."*

Moses is Delivered by God
A Hebrew couple gave birth to a son in the midst of an Egyptian mandate given by Pharaoh to kill all male babies. Pharaoh, the king of Egypt, was alarmed at how fast the Hebrews were growing. In a twist of fate, Pharaoh's own daughter found Moses, who had been hidden in a basket by his parents on the banks of the Nile River. Pharaoh's daughter adopted Moses, and he was welcomed into the royal family. He was also given an Egyptian education, which was the best of the day, as Stephen tells us in his sermon in Acts (7:22).

Moses On the Run
Moses' heart was always with his people, though. His fellow Hebrews were slaves of the Egyptians and were treated cruelly. One day Moses killed an Egyptian for beating a Hebrew slave mercilessly. To escape judgment, Moses ran away and hid in the desert of Midian. Moses stayed for forty years and married his wife there.

Moses Is Called by God
While working for his father-in-law, God appeared to Moses in a burning bush, and Moses was commissioned to deliver the Israelites from Pharaoh. Moses was one of the most revered leaders of the Old Testament. His accomplishments are many. Here are a few:
- He was used by God to perform miracles. The ten plagues that gave Israel their freedom were all done through Moses.
- The last plague became known as "Passover" and is still celebrated by Jews to this day. It is mentioned fifty times in the Old Testament.
- He was a prophet.
- He was a lawgiver.
- He wrote the first five books of the Bible.
- He led 2.5 million Hebrews to the border of their new homeland: Israel.

TOPIC 2: FROM EGYPT TO SINAI—EXODUS 14-19
The greatest miracle of Israel's existence occurs in chapter 14. God opened the Red Sea for the Israelites to pass through and closed it when the Egyptian army entered it and drowned them. Israel was now free from Egypt. Israel now traveled to Mount Sinai, where God had first appeared to Moses during his days on the run.

TOPIC 3: THE GIVING OF THE LAW—EXODUS 20-24
Spectacular cosmic signs frightened the Israelites as they prepared themselves for God's arrival on Mount Sinai. Moses met with God on the mount for forty days and nights. God gave the Ten Commandments and other laws to Moses. The laws include:
- The rights of persons
- The rights of property
- How to be right with God
- The blessings if Israel obeyed

In all, 619 commands were given. The commands were Israel's spiritual, civic, and personal responsibilities before their holy God.

TOPIC 4: THE TABERNACLE—EXODUS 25-40
In this section, Israel is commissioned to build a sanctuary for God to dwell in. The place would be called the *tabernacle*, which means "to dwell." This portable place of worship and sacrifice would serve Israel for four hundred years until the first permanent house of God, the temple, was built by King Solomon. God gave Moses precise instructions for building the tabernacle, which were to be followed exactly. The materials and colors used in the structure are all symbolic. Here are a few:
- Purple—royalty
- Red—sacrifice for sin
- Blue—heaven
- Fine linen—righteousness
- Incense—prayer
- Gold—deity
- Silver—redemption

The gold, silver, and linen were probably given to Israel by the Egyptians before their exodus. Exodus is a picture of salvation. We were slaves to sin as the people of Israel were slaves in Egypt. We were delivered miraculously by the cross and resurrection. They were delivered by the ten plagues and the Red Sea miracle. God rightfully desires our worship. Israel built the tabernacle to facilitate worship. Our promised land is heaven. For the Hebrews, it was the land of Israel.

Leviticus
The Book of Worship

OUTLINE
1. The Way to God (1–10)
2. The Way to Fellowship with God (11–27)

INTRODUCTION
The original title of Leviticus is: "Pertaining to the Levites."
The central message:
1. God expects worship.
2. We need to be taught how to worship.

FAST FACTS
- The author is Moses. The book was written about 1444 BC.
- It was a "handbook of instruction" for the Levitical priests of Israel.
- The theme is "holiness and sanctification." This theme is stated 130 times.
- The words *purity* and *clean* are used more than 200 times in Leviticus.
- Holiness means "to be separate."
- In the Old Testament, the only way to God was through sacrifice as atonement for sin. In fact, in the first seven chapters, sacrifices and offerings are mentioned two hundred times.

THE WAY TO GOD—LEVITICUS 1–10
There are five basic offerings in Leviticus:
1. **The Burnt Offering:** Leviticus 1:1–9—a burnt offering of a male animal prescribed daily, weekly, and monthly for the sins of individuals and of Israel as a whole
2. **The Grain Offering:** Leviticus 2:1–16—an oven-baked cake—encouraged sacrifice regardless of economic and social circumstances

3. **The Fellowship Offering:** Leviticus 3:1–17—an animal burned on the altar—was a meal given to the Lord because of sin
4. **The Sin Offering:** Leviticus 4:1–5, 13—for unintentional sins—no restitution was required
5. **The Trespass Offering:** Leviticus 5:14–6:7—for accidentally erring with the tithe (forgetting)—eating parts of sacrifice belonging to priest—hurting a neighbor (lying, stealing, cheating)

Laws for Priests: Leviticus 8–10
To represent the people, the priest was:
- Washed, sin-free, Leviticus 10–11
- Specifically dressed, fit to worship, Leviticus 5–9
- Dipped in blood, which signified total dedication, Leviticus 8:23, 24

The people of Israel had to go through the priest to communicate with God.

THE WAY TO FELLOWSHIP WITH GOD—LEVITICUS 11–27

Laws of Purity: Leviticus 11–22
- Concerning food—birds, fish, insects
- Physical health is our duty

Laws of Feasts (or, Festivals): Leviticus 23–24
- Passover
- Unleavened Bread
- Firstfruits
- Pentecost

Laws of Soil and Soul: Leviticus 25–26
- Sabbatical Year–Israel was to work six years, then take one off to rest the land and rest from labor.
- Jubilee Year–fiftieth year celebration–liberty
  1. Debts were done away with
  2. Slaves who sold themselves into service in an effort to pay off their debts were set free
  3. Property was given back to the original owner

The Law of the Voluntary Vow: Leviticus 27
These were special laws for any voluntary dedication to Yahweh (the name for God which means "I Am") of people, homes, fields, firstborn, etc.

Leviticus is a book that appears tedious with all of its details. Because of our sin problem, which blocks us from God, purity and holiness were achieved through sacrifice. God desires our worship, and He is our instructor. Not until Jesus became our sacrifice on the cross and rose from the dead did the Old Testament system become unnecessary. Israel, the new nation of God, was a theocratic kingdom. In other words, God was their leader and not a human king. Later on, the people demanded a human king, like the other nations. This proved to be a huge mistake. God wanted their lives to revolve around Him and not a king's. This was reflected by the tabernacle, which was positioned in the center of Israel's camp. The Most Holy Place, or Holy of Holies, was in the center of the tabernacle. This continually illustrated the centrality of God in the people's lives.

Jesus Christ is the fulfillment of the Old Testament sacrificial system.
But when Christ came as high priest of the good things that are now already here, he went through the greater and more perfect tabernacle that is not made with human hands, that is to say, is not a part of this creation. He did not enter by means of the blood of goats and calves; but he entered the Most Holy Place once for all by his own blood, thus obtaining eternal redemption. The blood of goats and bulls and the ashes of a heifer sprinkled on those who are ceremonially unclean sanctify them so that they are outwardly clean. How much more, then, will the blood of Christ, who through the eternal Spirit offered himself unblemished to God, cleanse our consciences from acts that lead to death, so that we may serve the living God! (Hebrews 9:11–14)

OLD TESTAMENT

Numbers
The Book of Wanderings

OUTLINE
1. The Organization at Mount Sinai (1–14)
2. The Disorganization in the Wilderness (15:1–20:21)
3. The Reorganization at the Jordan River (20:22–36:13)

INTRODUCTION
The book of Numbers deals with a forty-year period of Israel's history, in which Israel wandered in the desert needlessly because of their unbelief. God promised them the land of Canaan; yet the people who already lived in the land frightened Israel, so the Israelites waited and wandered.

FAST FACTS
- Moses is the author.
- The title written in Hebrew is "in the wilderness."
- Numbers is a book of organization.
- The book of Numbers picks up where Exodus ends. It was written between 1450 and 1410 BC.
- In the New Testament, believers are warned about unbelief, and Numbers is used as the illustration.
- The book covers the main events of the forty years and is considered one of the low points of Israel's history.
- Four titles for the book would all apply: Murmurings, Wanderings, Training, and Numbers.
- The book illustrates the tragedy of not trusting God: When we live in unbelief, we miss out on blessings God has for us. This is the way of our flesh.
- The Israelites wandered and complained for forty years. One of the easiest ways to tell that you are out of fellowship with God is when you complain. God calls us to a life of gratitude, not whining.

THE ORGANIZATION AT MOUNT SINAI—NUMBERS 1-14

God called Moses to take a census to see how many fighting men were available. The men had to be at least twenty years old. There were 603,550 men counted.

Next, God positioned every family within their tribes around the tabernacle.

Five families were to be consumed with work and service in and around the tabernacle. They were:
- the priests, who were assigned the tasks of worship, prayer, and intercession on behalf of the people
- the Levites, who were given to serve the priests
- the Kohathites, who were given the responsibility of moving the pieces of furniture within the tabernacle, such as the ark of the covenant
- the Gershonites, who were given the responsibility of the curtains and the coverings when the tabernacle was moved
- the Merarites, who were in charge of the boards, sockets, and solid parts of the tabernacle when moving camp

After the numbering and arranging of the people, God instructed the people on purity and worship. Israel began to complain about the food God had miraculously provided. Soon Moses' brother, Aaron, and sister, Miriam, joined in the verbal assaults on Moses and on God Himself.

At Kadesh Barnea, the people asked God to let them send spies into the land to check it out. Deuteronomy 1:22 tells us that the idea came from the people and not from God. Ten spies returned afraid and unwilling to proceed. Two spies trusted God and wanted to move forward. The people rebelled and were unwilling to go into the land God had promised them, so God gave them a forty-year sentence to wander in the desert—one year for each day that the spies were in the land. Ten of the spies took their eyes off of God and worried about the giants in the land. Joshua and Caleb were the two faithful spies who believed in God's promise to inhabit the land and that He had the power over the size of the people who lived there.

THE DISORGANIZATION IN THE WILDERNESS—NUMBERS 15–20:21

This section catalogs Israel's rebellions during their wanderings and God's judgments that followed. Korah's rebellion occurs during this time.

THE REORGANIZATION AT THE JORDAN RIVER—NUMBERS 20:22–36:13

The final section of Numbers prepares the nation for the entrance into the land. Even though Israel wandered for forty years, God never gave up on them. The Israelites began to develop an attitude problem that led to their unbelief. Once they lost their desire for the things of God, they lost their confidence in God's ability. God's judgment for this was to let a whole generation of unbelievers die in the desert. The new generation of Israelites would proceed into the land with a firm faith in God.

Deuteronomy
The Book of Second Law

OUTLINE
1. Moses' First Message (1–4)
2. Moses' Second Message (5–26)
3. Moses' Third Message (27–30)
4. Moses' Last Days (31–34)

INTRODUCTION

The book of Deuteronomy is a summary book for the previous forty years of the nation of Israel. Exodus, Leviticus, and Numbers are reviewed in this last book that Moses wrote. (Joshua wrote the last chapter concerning Moses' death.) This is a book of transition as Israel was poised at the edge of the land that God had promised they would one day possess.

FAST FACTS

- Deuteronomy comes from two Greek words: *Deutero*, meaning "second," and *nomos*, meaning "law."
- This book is referred to as the second law, as Moses applied its teaching to the people of Israel.
- The theme is "the motive of our obedience." Deuteronomy was written about 1407 BC.
- In Deuteronomy, the word "love" is used twenty-two times.
- The elder statesman Moses had a final message for the Israelites he had led for forty years. It was this: "Love God." Obedience is best when it results from an overflowing heart of love for God.

MOSES' FIRST MESSAGE—DEUTERONOMY 1–4

This section is a review of Israel's history. Moses charged the new generation to love God as they proceeded into the land.

MOSES' SECOND MESSAGE—DEUTERONOMY 5-26

This larger section of the book restated the Law given at Mount Sinai. Moses gave an in-depth explanation and application of the first commandment: "You shall have no other gods before me" (Exodus 20:3).

Moses also spoke of regulations for when the people entered the land of Israel. He also reminded them of the importance of appointing judges and gave instructions for priests and prophets. Moses also spoke of family life and the authority of fathers within the family.

MOSES' THIRD MESSAGE—DEUTERONOMY 27-30

In this section, Moses, the greatest prophet of God, preached his last sermon to Israel. It was prophetic in nature. He impressed on the nation the foolishness of disobedience. Israel would struggle with a disobedient spirit throughout its existence.

MOSES' LAST DAYS—DEUTERONOMY 31-34

Moses handed the leadership of Israel over to Joshua. He gave a final charge to the people and promised that God would go before them and never forsake them. He reminded Joshua and the priests of their responsibilities and predicted that Israel would fall away from God.

When Moses was finished, God took him to the top of Mount Nebo in present-day Jordan and showed him the land of Israel that the Hebrew people would now possess. Joshua would lead them there, and Moses would stay behind to die on that mountain at 120 years old. God kept Moses from entering the land because of his sin of pride in the wilderness, recounted in Numbers 20:9-13. Yet, God Himself wrote of Moses' greatness as He closed the Pentateuch (the five books of the law) with these words:

Since then, no prophet has risen in Israel like Moses, whom the LORD knew face to face, who did all those miraculous signs and wonders the LORD sent him to do in Egypt—to Pharaoh and to all his officials and to his whole land. For no one has ever shown the mighty power or performed the awesome deeds that Moses did in the sight of all Israel. (Deuteronomy 34:10-12)

Joshua
The Book of Possession

OUTLINE
1. The Call (1)
2. The Crossing (2–4)
3. The Cleansing (5)
4. The Conquest (6–11)
5. The Counting (12–24)

INTRODUCTION

This book is actually the account of the military campaign to conquer the land of Canaan. The Pentateuch leads up to Canaan, and the book of Joshua leads into Canaan. The next twelve books are called the Historical Books. They describe Israel's settlement in the land. Joshua, then, is the connecting link between the Pentateuch and the historical books.

FAST FACTS
- The author and chief character of the book is Joshua.
- The book shows how faith, obedience, and loyalty are essential for receiving God's blessing.
- The title Joshua means "Jehovah is salvation." The New Testament name in Greek is "Jesus."
- It was written between 1400 and 1370 BC.
- Joshua was born a slave in Egypt.
- At the exodus he was forty years old.
- At the age of eighty he was appointed Moses' successor.
- He lived until he was 110.

Five Striking Parallels: Joshua and Ephesians
- Each book gives an inheritance: Joshua—earthly; Ephesians—spiritual.

- Each inheritance was opened by a divinely ordained leader: Joshua—Joshua; Ephesians—Jesus.
- Each inheritance was a gift from God to be received by faith.
- Each inheritance was based on God's revelation given to His children.
- Each book is a scene in the midst of conflict.

Joshua exhibited some wonderful traits as the Spirit of God worked in his life:
- Wisdom—he made major decisions every day!
- Preparation—he served under Moses for forty years.
- Courage—he was brave in the midst of great conflict.
- Seeker of God's will—he didn't see God's face, as Moses did but he had to go through a chief priest which was more difficult.
- Faith—he did what had never been done.

THE CALL—JOSHUA 1

God promised that He would be with Joshua as He was with Moses. God charged Joshua to be strong and courageous and to lead the people into the land. God gave Joshua a mandate for success in Joshua 1:8: "Keep this Book of the Law always on your lips; meditate on it day and night, so that you may be careful to do everything written in it. Then you will be prosperous and successful."

The parameters of the land God gave to Israel include present-day Lebanon, Syria, and Jordan.

THE CROSSING—JOSHUA 2–4

Joshua and all of the Israelites crossed the Jordan River. The ark of the covenant went before the people, leading them through the Jordan River. God performed one more miracle for the new nation as He dried up the river, which was at flood stage, when the priests' feet touched the water's edge.

THE CLEANSING—JOSHUA 5

Circumcision was a physical act that identified the men of Israel as God's own. Since those males born in the forty-year desert wandering had not been circumcised, God commanded this to be done before they conquered the land.

THE CONQUEST—JOSHUA 6–11
The first city to fall was Jericho. It is the oldest city in the whole world.[13] God commanded Joshua to march around the city for six days before the final march on the seventh day. On the last day, the Israelites were commanded to march around the walls of Jericho seven times. After the trumpet blasted and the people shouted, the walls crumbled; and Israel took Jericho with ease.

The rest of the section chronicles the miraculous hand of God in establishing Israel in the land.

THE COUNTING—JOSHUA 12–24
The second half of the book detailed the division of the land of Canaan, now called Israel. Joshua, Israel's greatest general, died at 110 and is buried in the hill country of Ephraim. Joshua is a profile in courage and utter dependency on God. He is remembered as one of Israel's greatest leaders ever.

Old Testament

Judges
The Book of Complacency

OUTLINE
1. The Apostasy Commenced (1–3:4)
2. The Apostasy Contested (3:5–16:31)
3. The Apostasy Characterized (17–21)

INTRODUCTION

Judges contains parts of Israel's history from the days of Joshua until Israel's first king. It covers a period of about 350 years. As the book of Joshua closes, we find Israel partially established in the land. Districts were divided into the twelve tribes. Yet God told Joshua in 13:1 that land remained to be possessed. The unconquered Canaanites lived in the center of the land. As a result, the northern district and southern district were separated from the rest of the land. Rather than finish the job, they rested because of a spirit of complacency.

FAST FACTS

- The author of the book has never been established. The one that seems logical is Samuel.
- Judges was written about 1000 BC.
- The theme is "obedience results in blessing."
- The book of Judges shows the consequences of half-hearted obedience.
- God's people began to assimilate with the Canaanites, picking up their
  - languages
  - religions
  - culture in general.
- Instead of a united nation, the Israelites resembled a loose confederacy.
- They were easy prey to small rebel groups.
- It is perhaps the darkest period in Hebrew history.
- The book begins with compromise and ends in anarchy and confusion.

- Judges is a book that links different forms of leadership together in Israel's history:
  - Joshua—leader and shepherd
  - Judges—military and civic leader
  - Ruth/Samuel—prophet and finally a king
- Rebellion is seen in the philosophy of the day: *"everyone did as they saw fit"* (Judges 17:6 and 21:25).
- J. Sidlow Baxter sums up Judges this way: *"Would that we might erase from the tablets of Israel's history the many dark doings and sad happenings which make up the bulk of this seventh book of the canon. But alas, the sin of Israel is written 'with a pen of iron and with the point of a diamond.'"*[14]
- God's philosophy regarding nations, as found in Proverbs 14:34, is simple: He sees them as one of two things—righteous or sinful.
- Judges contains leaders of three differing backgrounds:
  - Warrior
  - Prophet
  - Priest
- Of the thirteen leader-judges, we find no one whom we would consider great.
- Each leader has strengths, yet each of them has a peculiarity.

A picture of Judges would resemble a wheel. In twenty-one chapters, the wheel spun seven times.

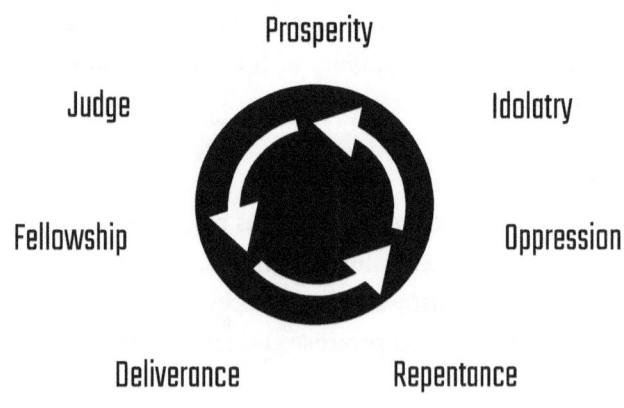

THE APOSTASY COMMENCED—JUDGES 1-3:4

Judges begins with a clear void of leadership. Israel had been under the direction of General Joshua, but now he rested with his fathers and was buried at age 110. As the book begins, Israel is unclear about who to follow now and how to proceed. Spiritually, things go from good to bad in one generation. Judges 2:10 sets the tone for the rest of the book with these words: *"After that whole generation had been gathered to their ancestors, another generation grew up, who knew neither the LORD nor what he had done for Israel."* The stage was set for a national collapse.

Israel was in the north of the land and the south of the land. The Canaanites were placed in between. Since Israel did not drive out the pagans, they were influenced by them. Soon they adopted their ways and became idol worshippers.

THE APOSTASY CONTESTED—JUDGES 3:5-16:31

Deborah will always be remembered as a mother who saved Israel from the Canaanites. Male leadership was so weak in those days that she had acted as a military general in the great battle on Mount Tabor.

Gideon stands out as an example of a man who trusted in Yahweh alone for victory. God reduced Gideon's army from 32,000 to 300 so that He alone would be glorified and not Gideon. The Midianites were defeated as God led Gideon's army in a night raid against the mighty pagan army.

Samson stands out as an example of someone who was spiritual one day and ungodly the next. In his leadership, he was occasionally filled with the Spirit. In Samson's final hours, he gave his life while collapsing the support pillars of a pagan Philistine temple in Gaza. In his death, he killed more Philistines than in his life. In the New Testament, the Holy Spirit is seen in believers' lives as permanent and not temporary, as in Samson's.

Baal worship was evil idolatry that often included human sacrifice to the Canaanite god. Asherah poles, another pagan example, were part of the Phoenician and Syrian culture, which was sensual, lewd, and immoral. Sadly, both of these pagan practices became a part of Israel during the period of the Judges.

THE APOSTASY CHARACTERIZED—JUDGES 17–21

The last section of Judges tells us how widespread idolatry and paganism had deeply embedded its roots into Israel's soil. Judges 17:6 says, *"Everyone did as they saw fit."* This theme characterized Israel for three and a half centuries.

Book Uniqueness - Joshua and Judges Compared	
Joshua	**Judges**
Victory	Defeat
Freedom	Slavery
Faith	Unbelief
Progress	Decline
Spiritual Vision	Earthly Involvement
Allegiance to the LORD	Apostasy from the LORD
Joy	Sorrow
Strength	Weakness
Unity	Anarchy
Sin Judged	Sin Ignored

Old Testament

Ruth
The Book of Love

OUTLINE
1. The Decision of Faith (1)
2. The Provision of Faith (2)
3. The Intention of Faith (3)
4. The Compensation of Faith (4)

INTRODUCTION

This little book is a love story, yet the word *love* is never used! Biblical love always springs from a commitment. Although the book of Ruth describes the deep love between a man and a woman, it shows that marital love involves the whole family, even in-laws.

The events of this book occur during the period of the judges. The time of the judges in the history of Israel is marked by apostasy, yet this book is like a little oasis of faithfulness. The book also gives us a glimpse into the life of some ordinary people. Ruth was a Gentile married to a Jew!

Ruth gives a partial lineage of David and Christ and shows that Gentile blood was in the line of the Messiah. The author is unknown, but many suggest it to be Samuel. Boaz, who married Ruth, is known as a kinsman redeemer. He is an Old Testament picture of Christ in many ways:
1. He was a blood relative. (Romans 1:3; Hebrews 2:14)
2. He had the ability to pay. (1 Peter 1:18–19)
3. He was a willing redeemer. (Hebrews 10:7)

FAST FACTS
- Ruth means "friend" or "associate" and was most likely written by Samuel although it has not been confirmed. The book was written between 1375 and 1050 BC.

- Ruth is one of two books named after a woman in the Bible, the other being Esther.
- Ruth was a Moabite living among Hebrews. In contrast, Esther was a Hebrew living among Persians.
- Since this is a book of redemption based on a love story, it's easy to see why in God's eyes, redemption is the highest form of love.
- The most frequent mention of God in the book is in the prayers it contains.
- Ruth shows a hopeless situation. Yet the phrase "may the LORD," which occurs over and over in the prayers, shows that God is our only hope.
- Ruth's miraculous ability to conceive (4:13) is another example of God's involvement.
- Ruth was the great grandmother of King David. Above all, she was selected to be in the line of the coming Messiah.

THE DECISION OF FAITH—RUTH 1

Because of a famine, an Israelite family moved to Moab for ten years. The Moabites were infamous enemies of Israel. They were the descendants of an incestuous relationship between Lot and his daughter (Genesis 19).

Ruth was a Moabite. Even though Moab was thoroughly pagan, Ruth was a faithful, determined woman of God. She married a son of the Israelite family, who later died. Since her husband's mother, Naomi, was also a widow, Ruth stayed with her and traveled with her back to Israel.

THE PROVISION OF FAITH—RUTH 2

Naomi had a relative back in Bethlehem named Boaz. He was a man of great standing within the community. He was a spiritual man and was blessed financially. The meeting of Ruth and Boaz was orchestrated by God. Boaz was also blessed with a good personality. He greeted Ruth with these words: "The LORD be with you!" (v. 4)

THE INTENTION OF FAITH—RUTH 3

Naomi, Ruth's mother-in-law, played the matchmaker with Boaz. Boaz was the perfect gentleman to Ruth. He complimented her. He was concerned with ethics. He was concerned with Ruth's reputation. But as a male relative of Naomi, Boaz was also able to be a kinsman-redeemer and marry Ruth legally.

THE COMPENSATION OF FAITH—RUTH 4

The elders of the town gathered at the town gate to discuss the potential marriage of Boaz and Ruth. Since there was one male relative in line ahead of Boaz with the legal option to buy the land that her now-deceased husband had owned, Boaz approached him to redeem it. Boaz also declared his intention to marry Ruth. The man deferred to Boaz, and Boaz and Ruth were married. Ruth entered the Hebrew lineage that soon produced David, Israel's great king.

Some important lessons are learned in the book of Ruth:
- God always responds to faith.
- God always blesses commitment.
- God honors a proper view of love.
- Character is easily seen.
- A godly home is one of God's greatest gifts.

1 Samuel
The Book of Israel's first King

OUTLINE
1. Eli and Samuel (1–3)
2. The History of the Ark of the Covenant (4–7:1)
3. Samuel and Saul (7:2–15:35)
4. Saul and David (16–31)

INTRODUCTION
First Samuel leads into the three double books of the Old Testament. These three double books form a complete section. They record the rise, establishment, expansion, and fall of the Hebrew monarchy. In 1 Samuel, we see Israel change from a theocracy to a monarchy. The warrior-judges had passed, and a priest-judge named Eli had now come. He would be followed by a prophet-judge named Samuel. With Samuel, the period of the judges ends, and the order of the prophets begins. It is through the priest that the people draw near to God, and through the prophet that God draws near to the people.

FAST FACTS
- 1 Samuel was written by Samuel around 930 BC.
- The material in 1 Samuel is largely biographical, recording the lives of three very colorful personalities:
    › Samuel
    › Saul
    › David
- The books of 1 Samuel and 2 Samuel used to be one book, but the Greek Septuagint (circa 200 BC) divided them, along with 1 and 2 Kings and 1 and 2 Chronicles.
- The book covers a period of 120 years, from the birth of Samuel to the death of Saul.
- The book is historical and theological.

- The theme is "The people who live according to the covenant are blessed—the ones who don't are not."
- Examples of blessings are seen in the life of Samuel.
- Examples of blessings being removed are seen in Hophni and Phinehas.

It is in this book that we meet the famed "man after God's own heart," which can only refer to David. David was the shepherd boy who God transformed into the King of Israel.

ELI AND SAMUEL—1 SAMUEL 1–3

In the time when everyone did what was right in his or her own eyes, Hannah stands out as a woman of God. Elkanah, her husband, was typical of his time. On one hand, he would worship God at the tabernacle in Shiloh; yet, on the other hand, he also had two wives. This was a clear violation of the sixth commandment, "You shall not commit adultery" (Exodus 20:14).

Hannah wanted a child, and particularly a son. Her promise to God if He gave her a son was that he would be a Nazirite. The Nazirite vow, found in Numbers 6:1–8, was threefold:
- No haircut
- No wine
- No defilement by going near a dead person

Eli was the high priest at the time. (His two sons were also priests; yet both were ungodly.) When Hannah went to pray, Eli blessed Hannah and told her, *"May the God of Israel grant you what you have asked of him."* Eli had no idea that Elkanah and Hannah's son would be the next high priest, replacing his own wicked sons. Hannah made good on her promise and gave her son, Samuel, to the Lord for life. God called Samuel to be a prophet at a very young age, and he was recognized as a prophet by all of Israel.

THE HISTORY OF THE ARK—1 SAMUEL 4–7:1

The judgment of God came to Israel next as the Philistines killed Eli's sons and captured the ark of the covenant, the very centerpiece of the tabernacle. More than thirty thousand Israelites died in the battle. When Eli heard the news, he fell over and died. He had long ago given up on his sons, but hearing that the ark of the covenant was captured was more than Eli could handle.

SAMUEL AND SAUL—1 SAMUEL 7:2–15

Sadly, Samuel's sons became like Eli's—corrupt and ungodly. Israel asked for a king like the other nations (8:5). Israel gave up their belief that God was their leader and wanted a human leader.

Saul was an impressive-looking man to the Israelites. God selected him to be king even though he would only serve Yahweh half-heartedly. God forecast that Saul's kingdom would not endure. Israel demanded a king, and God answered their prayer with one. This proved to be a big mistake for the nation.

SAUL AND DAVID—1 SAMUEL 16–31

The Spirit of God had been transferred to the youngest son of Jesse—David, the shepherd boy. David killed the Philistine giant Goliath, and the whole nation celebrated. They even sang songs about their new hero. Saul, plagued by an evil spirit, was jealous of God's hand on David.

The rest of the book catalogs King Saul's murderous attempts on the life of David. Saul's son Jonathan made a pact with David to protect him from his own father. What made David great was that he accepted the trial of Saul's attempts on his life as a tool to shape his character. He learned. He grew. And he became Israel's greatest king after Saul died.

The book ends with Saul and his sons dying at the hands of the Philistines, thus wiping out Saul's descendants and his kingdom as God foretold. Even though Israel made the mistake of wanting a king, as the other nations of the world had, God would redeem this request in David, Israel's next king.

The Lord's Method of Training
1. Solitude – He was in silence alone with God and His creation. David was a man of God before he was on the throne. He had depth of character.
2. Obscurity – Nobody watched him. Nobody cared, yet he realized that God was there.
3. Monotony – He maintained the menial tasks, the tasks that never changed. David never seemed to experience embarrassment or reluctance – just faithfulness.
4. Reality – He was faithful where God put him. King qualities developed – courage, conviction, and strength of heart.

David Became:
- The giant killer – Whom no one else would fight.
- The teenaged king-elect – Selected over all his brothers and Saul's sons.
- The composer of Psalms – A man of the Word and God's inspiration flowed freely through him.
- Saul's personal musician – He soothed him.
- The friend of Jonathan, Saul's son.
- The hunted fugitive – Ran for years.
- The King of Israel – A good king.
- The father of the wisest man in the world – Solomon had it all.
- The champion in battle– Israel's greatest days!
- A man of glorious triumphs, yet great personal tragedy.
- Uniquely gifted but human to the core.
- In the Bible, 66 chapters are devoted to David.
- A principle worth remembering is this: God's choice of persons is contrary to human reason.

2 Samuel
The Book of King David

OUTLINE
1. David Pulls the Nation Together (1–7)
2. David Defeats Israel's Enemies (8–10)
3. Personal Sin—Public Revolution (11–20)
4. Final Deeds—Final Reflections (21–24)

INTRODUCTION

Second Samuel is all about David. In 1 Samuel we saw David rising while Saul was reigning, but now, in 2 Samuel, David is reigning. Second Samuel covers the time from David's anointing to just before his death, a period of about forty years. In that time, David encountered several triumphs and troubles. The theme of 2 Samuel is that success is turned to failure by sin. The parallel history is found in 1 Chronicles 11–29. In 2 Samuel, King David made Jerusalem the political and spiritual center of Israel. We see the establishment of the Davidic dynasty. David accumulated many military victories. We also see that David fell into his most infamous sin with Bathsheba. David also provoked God's displeasure when he, in a state of pride, numbered the people. Still, over and over it is pointed out that David's success was because of the recognized presence of Yahweh.

FAST FACTS
- The book was written around 930 BC by Samuel.
- In 1 Samuel 16:14, the Spirit of the Lord departed from Saul, and an evil spirit tormented him. At the same time, the Spirit of the Lord came upon David in power.
- In the Old Testament, the Holy Spirit was selective and temporary (e.g. *"The Spirit of the LORD came powerfully upon him so that he tore the lion apart with his bare hands as he might have torn a young goat,"* Judges 14:6).
- In the New Testament, the Holy Spirit is promised and permanent for all believers: *"For we were all baptized by one Spirit so as to form one*

body—whether Jews or Gentiles, slave or free—and we were all given the one Spirit to drink" (1 Corinthians 12:13).
- David's rise to the throne began with his defeat of Goliath. Shortly after this, Saul began to resent David and sought to kill him.
- David was spared by the promise of God that one day he would be on the throne.
- He was protected by:
  - Michal, Saul's daughter and his wife
  - Samuel the prophet
  - Jonathan, Saul's son.
- David had many chances to kill King Saul. Yet he had high regard for the Lord's anointed.
- Saul lowered himself to consulting a medium in the last days of his life.
- Second Samuel ends with David's men celebrating in victory and Saul's men falling in defeat.
- Saul was wounded in a battle with the Philistines; and fearing a cruel death, he took his own life as he threw himself on his own sword.

DAVID PULLS THE NATION TOGETHER—2 SAMUEL 1–7

King David's reign is proof that God can work through us even in the midst of our failings. David had many spiritual highs and many worldly lows. His colossal leap to the throne of Israel can only be explained by the almighty power of God. David had now gone from the number one fugitive in all of Israel to the ruler of the nation of God. To begin with, it is helpful to read Psalm 142, which David penned as he hid in a cave from King Saul, who wanted to kill him. That was during 1 Samuel. In 2 Samuel, however, King Saul was now dead; and David had no reason to hide anymore.

As 1 Samuel ends, a wounded King Saul takes his own life by falling on his sword. As 2 Samuel begins, a messenger brings the news to David that after Saul was wounded, he himself killed King Saul. This is clearly a lie, as the messenger is trying to earn favor with the new king of Israel. Not knowing that the servant's story is fabricated, David takes the man's life for lifting his hand against the Lord's anointed. What made it worse for the messenger was that he was an Amalekite. The Amalekites were avowed enemies of Israel, and this act disrespected Israel's king.

David mourned Saul's death and that of his best friend, Jonathan, whom he lost in the same battle. David began his reign by defeating Saul's descendants and also the Philistines again. Two of the most significant events in all of Israel's history happened in David's first few years as king. David captured Jerusalem, and it became Israel's capital city. Also, he brought the ark of the covenant to reside there.

DAVID DEFEATS ISRAEL'S ENEMIES—2 SAMUEL 8–10

David next defeated several of Israel's enemies and secured the nation in the process. Along the way, David showed incredible kindness to King Saul's grandson, who is Jonathan's son. In memory of Jonathan, David gave Mephibosheth back his father's land and honored him as a son allowing him to eat at David's royal table.

PERSONAL SIN TO PUBLIC REVOLUTION—2 SAMUEL 11–20

David's downfall begins with his adulterous affair with Bathsheba. He had her husband, a military man, killed in an effort to make himself look better. This was the king at perhaps his lowest moment. David greatly displeased the Lord, and his sin led to a disintegration of his family life. David's own son, Absalom, revolted and tried to steal the kingdom from his own father. The holy nation of God was in absolute chaos.

FINAL DEEDS—FINAL REFLECTIONS—2 SAMUEL 21–24

David was truly a man of contrast. He was called by God "a man after his own heart" (1 Samuel 13:14). He wrote numerous songs to God and is also referred to as "the singer of songs." He wrote scripture. He was also, without a doubt, Israel's greatest king. Yet, he fell apart morally. God continued to use him, though, as David had a soft heart and was always willing to repent. David's penitent spirit is seen clearly in his response to the prophet Nathan's rebuke of his sin with Bathsheba in 2 Samuel 12. David composed a song of repentance in Psalm 51 of the Psalter in review of his evil deed. David was far from perfect, but he experienced God's forgiveness because of his willingness to repent. David was a mighty tool in God's hand.

1 Kings
The Book of the Divided Kingdom

OUTLINE
1. Long Live the King (1–4)
2. The Temple (5–8)
3. The Covenant (9)
4. The Rise and Fall of Solomon (10–11)
5. The Divided Kingdom (12–22)

INTRODUCTION

First Kings and 2 Kings were originally in the Hebrew Bible as one book. The two books cover the time period from David's final days to the fall of the kingdom of Israel. In 1 Kings, we see the nation of Israel at its zenith. First Kings records the building of the temple. Second Kings records the burning of the temple. In 1 Kings and 2 Kings, we see prophetic foreshadowing of New Testament truth. Examples include:
- Solomon's reign—someday a greater son of David will reign, namely Jesus Christ (Revelation 20)
- Visit of the Queen of Sheba—a picture of a sinner seeking to know God and His wisdom (John 3)
- Elijah being caught up to heaven; this is a preview of the rapture (1 Thessalonians 4)

FAST FACTS
- Jewish tradition holds that the author was Jeremiah.
- The title—Kings—was chosen since it is a systematic record of Israel's kings. The book was written about 550 BC.
- The difference between Kings and Chronicles:
  - Kings—a political view
  - Chronicles—a spiritual view
- The central character of 1 Kings is Solomon.

Speaking of Solomon:
- Under Solomon, Jerusalem glistened like a brilliant gem, the central stone of the empire for forty years.
- Jerusalem was "the city set on a hill" that influenced the whole Middle East region.
- The reports were incredible. Solomon's reputation was such that a queen traveled thousands of miles from Africa just to verify the reports she had heard about him.
- Jesus spoke of the splendor of Solomon in his glory and the greatness of his wisdom in the Sermon on the Mount!

LONG LIVE THE KING—1 KINGS 1–4

David on his deathbed gave a blessing to Solomon. Bathsheba, the woman that David unlawfully took to be his wife, had birthed Solomon, and he became Israel's third king. God can glorify Himself even in the midst of our own sin and failure. Solomon is often shown with "his seams falling apart," yet early on we see an eager, godly king with incredible gifts on the throne of Israel. He
- authored three thousand proverbs
- composed more than a thousand songs
- administrated all of Israel
- built homes, reservoirs, gardens, orchards, and vineyards
- diplomatically built alliances with many nations
- greatly improved business and trade relations

Solomon was, most importantly, a man of God. Second Chronicles 1:1 says: "Solomon son of David established himself firmly over his kingdom, for the LORD his God was with him and made him exceedingly great."

THE TEMPLE—1 KINGS 5–8

The monumental task of building the temple was given to King Solomon. His father, David, wanted to build it, but because he was a man of bloodshed, God gave the high honor to his son Solomon. The project took seven years and more than 180,000 men to complete. That Solomon could direct and coordinate this entire workforce was a feat in itself.

The temple that Solomon built lasted four hundred years. The God-given dimensions were double that of the tabernacle, which was Israel's portable meeting place with God. The temple was built on Mount Moriah, the place where Abraham was going to sacrifice Isaac. King David later purchased this area from Araunah. Solomon was the most respected king on earth. Men from all over the world were sent by their kings to learn from Solomon. He accomplished many things in life, but they pale in comparison to his building of the great temple of God. First Kings 8:10–13 describes the miracle of God descending from heaven and residing in the temple. The "Shekinah" Glory of God came to the temple upon its completion.

THE COVENANT—1 KINGS 9

The covenant made to Solomon was conditional, meaning he had obligations to fulfill or the promises from God would be voided. Solomon and sons had to walk with God and reject idolatry. If they failed, God would cut Israel off from the land and reject the glorious temple.

THE RISE AND FALL OF SOLOMON—1 KINGS 10–11

Solomon's wisdom was so vast that the queen of Sheba came from Africa to ask him questions. Chapter 10 says that she was overwhelmed by Solomon. King Solomon's downfall stemmed from his love of foreign women of pagan countries. More than seven hundred wives and three hundred concubines led him away from God and caused him to fall in fulfilling his part of the covenant laid out in chapter 9.

THE DIVIDED KINGDOM—1 KINGS 12–22

The kingdom split, and idolatry grew. God raised up Elijah as a prophet due to the ungodly leaders. Elijah faithfully stood for God and was used by God to do the miraculous. His showdown with the prophets of Baal proved conclusively that Yahweh, the God of Israel, was the true God.

2 Kings
The Book of the Kingdom's Collapse

 **OUTLINE**
1. The Corruption of the Divided Kingdom (1–16)
2. The Results of the Divided Kingdom (17–25)

INTRODUCTION
This book is the tragic account of Israel's kingdom era. Idolatry and moral failure characterized the nation. Judgment would soon follow. When the people sought the gods of idolatry, moral bankruptcy was not far behind. God would use the Assyrians to attack the northern kingdom of Israel in 722 BC. In 586 BC the Babylonians would drag the southern kingdom of Judah into captivity. The prophecies of Deuteronomy 28:15-32 would be fulfilled because of idolatry. The prophecy of a fallen kingdom was given to King Solomon in 1 Kings 9:4-9, and this would be realized. The kingdom had been divided in two for about one hundred years by now. God warned the people for another 125 years before the kingdom collapsed.

FAST FACTS
- The author of 2 Kings is unknown—Jewish tradition points to Jeremiah.
- The books of 1 Kings and 2 Kings were originally one book, written about 550 BC.
- The theme is "prolonged sin will bring ruin without remedy."

THE CORRUPTION OF THE DIVIDED KINGDOM—2 KINGS 1–16
The kingdom in disarray was also known for two prophets who were used by God Israel to perform some of the most spectacular miracles ever. Elijah was the prophet moving off the scene. The mantle of leadership in 2 Kings was passed to Elisha. The dramatic removal of Elijah straight to heaven in a chariot of fire opens chapter 2. Elijah and Enoch are the only two Old Testament saints who did not die but rather were translated directly to heaven.

Miracles of Elijah and Elisha were against Baal, the false god worshiped by many Israelites. Baal was the god of rain, fire, and farm crops. He also demanded child sacrifice. Elijah's and Elisha's miracles repeatedly showed the power of the true God over the purported realm of Baal, as well as the value God places on the life of a child.

In chapters 9 and 10, King Ahab's family was killed, including his evil wife, Jezebel. Ahab was a Baal worshipper. His successor, King Jehu, outdid Ahab in idolatry.

THE RESULTS OF THE DIVIDED KINGDOM—2 KINGS 17–25

The northern kingdom of Israel fell to the wicked kingdom of Assyria in chapter 17. The last kings feverishly attempted to block this, but to no avail. During this time, Jews married pagan Assyrians and other people groups. This began the Samaritan race, which the Jews detested. As half-breeds, Samaritans were considered second-class Israelites.

King Hezekiah was a bright spot in this otherwise dark history. His prayer to have his life spared from an otherwise terminal illness was answered. Though God added fifteen years to his life, King Hezekiah fathered Manasseh, who became Judah's worst king. The Babylonian captivity was launched in three waves, as described in chapter 24. The dream was over—Israel's kingdom was destroyed.

1st and 2nd Kings Compared	
1 Kings	**2 Kings**
Starts with King David	Ends with the King of Babylon
Solomon's Glory	Jehoiakim's Shame
Blessings of Obedience	Curse of Disobedience
Building of Temple	Burning of Temple
Beginning of Apostasy	Consequences of Apostasy
Kings Failed to Rule	Consequences of Failure to Rule
Elijah Prominent	Elisha Prominent
Long Suffering of God	Punishment from God

Elijah

Miracle	Reference	Factors
Food brought by ravens	1 Kings 17:5-6	Food
Widow's Food Multiplied	1 Kings 17:12-16	Flour and Oil
Widow's son raised to life	1 Kings 17:17-24	Life of a Child
Alter and sacrifice consumed	1 Kings 18:16-46	Fire and Water
Ahaziah's soldiers consumed	2 Kings 1:9-14	Fire
Jordan River parted	2 Kings 2:6-8	Water
Transported to heaven	2 Kings 2:11-12	Fire and Wind

Elisha

Miracle	Reference	Factors
Jordan River parted	2 Kings 2:13-14	Water
Spring purified at Jericho	2 Kings 2:19-22	Water
Widow's oil multiplied	2 Kings 4:1-7	Oil
Dead boy raised to life	2 Kings 4:18-37	Life of a child
Poison in stew purified	2 Kings 4:38-41	Flour
Prophets' food multiplied	2 Kings 4:42-44	Bread and grain
Naaman healed of leprosy	2 Kings 5:1-14	Water
Gehazi became leprous	2 Kings 5:15-27	Words alone
Ax-head floated	2 Kings 6:1-7	Water
Aramean army blinded	2 Kings 6:8-23	Elisha's prayer

OLD TESTAMENT

1 and 2 Chronicles
The Books of the Temple

> OUTLINE
> 1. The Genealogies (1 Chronicles 1–9)
> 2. The Reign of David (1 Chronicles 10–29)
> 3. The Reign of Solomon (2 Chronicles 1–9)
> 4. The Reigns of the Kings of Judah (2 Chronicles 10–36)

INTRODUCTION

Like the books of Samuel and Kings, the Chronicles were originally one book appearing at the end of the Hebrew Bible. The Hebrew title is "The Words of the Days," meaning events of the times.

The Chronicles begin with Adam and end with the decree of Cyrus in 536 BC. They embrace the whole sweep of Bible history, covering a period of more than 3,500 years. The time period from Adam to David is recounted in the form of genealogies; the period from David to the captivities is in the form of extended histories.

The stories of the two books center around the temple. The chief matter in the history of David's reign, according to Chronicles, was his abundant preparation for the building of the temple. The major part of the account of Solomon's reign is taken up with the building of the temple and its dedication. In the rest of the history, the largest space is given to the kings who introduced reformation and brought the people back to the temple and its services. In Chronicles, the temple is spoken of as "the house of God" or "the house of the LORD" thirty-four times.

This ignores the fact that the Chronicles were written for the restored Jews who had returned to Judea. Their homecoming was, in a sense, a hollow triumph, for they had no king. It was for this generation that the Chronicles

were compiled to remind them of three things:
1. That although the Davidic throne was not among them, the Davidic line was.
2. That apostasy had brought ruin and, therefore, the past was pregnant with lessons for the present.
3. That Jehovah was with them. He had brought them back and had enabled them to rebuild the temple.

The nation, therefore, must read its past, present, and future from the divine perspective. What Deuteronomy is to the rest of the Pentateuch and what John is to the Synoptics, Chronicles is to the history of Israel in Samuel and Kings.

FAST FACTS
- Many different sources are mentioned in the Chronicles to which the compiler referred and from which he drew material under the guidance of the Holy Spirit. Tradition points to Ezra as the compiler.
- Strictly speaking, we should refer to a compiler rather than an author.
- First Chronicles 6:15 and 9:1 make it clear that the Chronicles were compiled after the Babylonian captivity/exile.
- The books were written about 450–425 BC.
- First Chronicles 3:19–24 shows that the books were compiled after the return from Babylon.
- Compare 2 Chronicles 36:22–23 with Ezra 1:1–2. Talmudists ascribe the composition of Chronicles to Ezra but the completion of the genealogical tables to Nehemiah.
- The Chronicles were then compiled after the Babylonian exile and were intended for the remnant that returned. This is an important fact to remember in the study of these books.

THE GENEALOGIES: 1 CHRONICLES 1–9
The seemingly endless genealogies of 1 Chronicles trace three lines of people. They are:
- the royal line of David
  1 Chronicles 1–3

- the line of the twelve tribes
  1 Chronicles 4–8
- the inhabitants of Jerusalem
  1 Chronicles 9

Comparison of Samuel and Chronicles

Samuel and Kings	Chronicles
Biographical	Statistical
Personal	Official
Perspective of the prophet	Perspective of the Priest
Emphasis on the throne	Emphasis on the temple
Indictment of the nation	Incitement of the nation
Civil and political history	Sacred ecclesiastical history
Includes the history of the Northern Kingdom	Includes the history of the Northern Kingdom

THE REIGN OF DAVID—1 Chronicles 10–29

The high points of King David's rule are covered in detail. David proved to be Israel's greatest king with 50 chapters written about him in the Old Testament. The book views David through the glorious event of the temple. Although David was strictly forbidden from building the temple, God used him to prepare the entire priestly leadership for it, and also to make the blueprints for it.

THE REIGN OF SOLOMON—2 Chronicles 1–9

Solomon, David's son and successor to the throne, is seen in 2 Chronicles as he relates to the temple. Given the high privilege of building the House of God, Solomon is seen in light of this great event in the life and history of Israel. The high point of the nation is recorded in 2 Chronicles 5 as Solomon dedicates the temple. The ark of the covenant is placed within it as the Feast of Tabernacles (or, Festival of Tabernacles) is celebrated. The most significant event of the kingdom occurs when the glory of the Lord descends in a cloud to fill the temple.

THE REIGNS OF THE KINGS OF JUDAH—2 CHRONICLES 10-36
The section alternates between times of reform under good kings, like Asa and Jehoshaphat, and times of degeneration under evil kings, like Joash.

Ezra
The Book of Restoration

OUTLINE
1. The First Return Under Zerubbabel (1–6)
2. The Second Return Under Ezra (7–10)

INTRODUCTION
Ezra, Nehemiah, and Esther complete the Historical Section of the Old Testament. These books belong to the post-captivity period of Hebrew history. Israel's history has included:
- exit from Egypt **(Exodus)**
- establishing God's law **(Leviticus–Deuteronomy)**
- entering the land **(Joshua)**
- encounters in the land **(Judges)**
- examples of faithfulness **(Ruth)**
- establishing a monarchy **(1 Samuel–2 Chronicles)**

And now the sinfulness of the nation is judged two ways by God:
1. The kingdom is torn in half because of Israel's disobedience.
2. The northern half of the kingdom (Israel) is carried off into captivity in Assyria. The southern half (Judah) is taken captive to Babylon.

Ezra now records Israel entering the land again. It is, therefore, part of the "post-exilic" period and thus the book records God's dealings with Israel after captivity. Haggai, Zechariah, and Malachi also wrote and ministered during this period. The books of Ezra and Nehemiah deal with "remnants" who returned to Jerusalem. The remnant signifies a rather small group who were faithful to Yahweh during captivity and desired to return to the promised land despite the prosperity that their foreign captors could provide. In contrast, many Israelites assimilated into the pagan culture and turned their backs on their spiritual heritage and their national history. Romans 9:6–9 reveals that not all of Israel were of the faith. The "Israel of God" were the true, believing Jews. (We find this same principle to be true of "Christians" in the church today also. It's obvious that not everyone who occupies a seat on Sunday mornings truly knows Christ.) Those who were not of the "Israel of God" after the seventy-year Babylonian captivity decided to stay rather than return to Palestine.

FAST FACTS

- Ezra was a descendant of Aaron, and his name means "help." He authored this book around 450–444 BC.
- The theme of the book is "The word of God is our basis for everything." Ten times the word of God is referred to. Second Timothy 3:16 tells us that *"all scripture is God-breathed and is useful."*
- The subject of Ezra is the first return to the land under Zerubbabel and the second return under Ezra.
- Despite this glorious opportunity to restore Israel to its former position through the rebuilding of the temple, Ezra faced opposition and internal problems.
- In Scripture, there are four temples mentioned:
    1. Solomon's temple.
    2. Zerubbabel's (Ezra's) temple, which was enlarged during Jesus' time and called Herod's temple
    3. The Tribulation temple
    4. The millennial temple.

THE FIRST RETURN UNDER ZERUBBABEL—EZRA 1–6

In chapter 1, God used a pagan king named Cyrus to allow his nation to return to its home. Romans 13:1 states that all "authorities" are established by God, and this is evidenced by the revelation that "the LORD moved the heart of Cyrus" (1:1). The list of returnees adds up to about thirty thousand. Later on, a figure of around fifty thousand is given due to the fact that women, children, and others, possibly from the northern captivity, accompanied them.

After the one-thousand-mile trip to the land, the people reinstated the sacrificial system. They had not worshiped Yahweh for seventy years! The younger people, who had never worshiped, shouted for joy. The older people, who remembered the glory days of Israel, wept with joy. Of course, Satan attacked the work with division among the people, yet the work was resumed in chapter 5. In chapter 6, the work was completed and dedicated.

THE SECOND RETURN UNDER EZRA—EZRA 7-10

Central to the return was a firm holding to the Word of God. Ezra, the priest, led the way as a model for any leader or teacher: "For Ezra had devoted himself to the study and observance of the Law of the Lord, and to teaching its decrees and laws in Israel" (7:10).

The personnel were selected and presented to the people. But in chapter 8, the people lapsed into sinful ways again. Ezra called them back with a time of confession. The kingdom was restored. The temple was rebuilt. Israel was home, and Yahweh alone was their King alone once more.

Nehemiah
The Book of Reconstruction

OUTLINE
1. Rebuilding the Wall (1–7)
2. Revival (8–13:3)
3. Repairing Spiritual Leaks (13:3–31)

INTRODUCTION

The book is largely autobiographical and is the last of the historical books chronologically. The Old Testament goes no farther. When the book of Nehemiah closed, there was silence so far as inspired history was concerned for four hundred years. There were no miracles, no prophets, and no voice from heaven. The incidents recorded in Nehemiah are the last historical events in the Old Testament.

Nehemiah centers our attention on the reconstruction of the fortified city and the establishment of civil authority. Thus, Nehemiah is more secular than Ezra, which was concerned primarily with the building of the temple.

FAST FACTS
- The author is Nehemiah, and he wrote the book between 445 and 432 BC.
- 538 BC: the return of Israel under Cyrus—Ezra 1:1, the Lord moved the heart of Cyrus!
- 50,000 people returned under Zerubbabel.
- 516 BC: the temple is completed (after twenty years).
- Ezra 6–7: there is a gap of fifty-eight years; the events of Esther probably occurred then.
- Ezra returned with a few thousand and restored religious functions.
- 445 BC: Nehemiah returned after Artaxerxes gave permission.
- 7 BC: Nehemiah was the governor. Ezra was priest.
- The title of the book means "Jehovah comforts." The theme is "reconstruction through prayer and work."

REBUILDING THE WALL—NEHEMIAH 1-7

Nehemiah is an Old Testament leader of leaders. He answers two fundamental questions for us from his life concerning leadership. They are:

Question: What is biblical leadership?
Answer: The ability to move people in God's direction.
Question: What is essential in leading?
Answer: Solving problems God's way.

This demands a holy life to lead by example.

Nehemiah began as a cupbearer to the king and ended up leading Israel as the governor of its capital city of Jerusalem. The time period was November 15–December 15, 446 BC. Nehemiah was in Susa, a major city of Assyria, which is in present-day Iran. The book begins with Nehemiah's two questions to a returnee from Jerusalem. "How is the remnant of people?" he asked. The answer was that they were in great trouble and in distress. "How is Jerusalem?" Defenseless and without a city wall was the answer to the second question.

Nehemiah's response in 1:4 to the devastating news is a model for all of us to follow. He
- **"wept"**—he did not hide his sadness
- **"mourned"**—for days he experienced his sadness
- **"fasted"**—for several days he took no food
- **"prayed"**—his prayer is recorded in verses 5–10.

God answered his prayer in King Artaxerxes. Nehemiah had displayed sadness in the presence of the king, which was forbidden, yet he could not conceal it. Remarkably the king allowed Nehemiah to go to Jerusalem with letters marked with his personal seal, to ensure safe passage.

Nehemiah's life is a textbook of godly leadership. Here are more key points from Nehemiah's life:

- The Lord selects His own leadership.
- Holy people respect the holiness of God.
- God responds to a broken, repentant heart.
- A godly man goes to God before he forms his plans.

Great Prayer/ Great Determination: Nehemiah's Problems and his Responses

Problems	Responses
Walls broken and gates burned (1:2-3)	Grief and prayer (1:4) & motivation of the people to rebuild (2:17-18)
False accusation of the workers (2:19)	Confidence that God would give them success (2:20)
Ridicule of the workers (4:1-3)	Prayer (4:4-5) and action (4:6)
Plot to attack the workers (4:1-3)	Prayer and action (4:9)
Physical exhaustion and threat of murder (4:10-12)	Clustering people by families with weapons (4:13, 16-18) and encouragement of the people (4:14, 20)
Economic crisis and greed (5:1-5)	Anger (5:6), reflection, rebuke (5:7), and action (5:7b-11)
Plan to assassinate (or at least harm) Nehemiah (6:1-2)	Refusal to cooperate (6:3)
Slander against Nehemiah (6:5-7)	Denial (6:8) and prayer (6:9)
Plot to discredit Nehemiah (6:13)	Refusal to cooperate (6:11-13) and prayer (6:14)
Tobiah moved into a temple storeroom (13:4-7)	Tossing out Tobiah's furniture (13:8)
Neglect of temple tithes and offering (13:10)	Rebuke (13:11a), assigning Levites to their posts (13:11b), and prayer (13:22)
Violation of the Sabbath by business activities (13:15-16)	Rebuke (13:17-18), posting of guards (13:19), and prayer (13:29)
Mixed marriages (13:23-24)	Rebuke (13:25-27), removal of a guilty priest (13:28), and prayer (13:29)

Nehemiah began with the weakest point in the city wall—the gates. The gates were the place of attack. To possess the gates meant to possess the city.

City Gates in the Bible
- City gates were shut at nighttime to keep enemies out. They were opened in the morning.
- The elders of the city conducted business there.
- Markets were held there.
- Important announcements were given at the gate.
- The gates refer to the power of the city. Jesus said the gates of Hades (hell) would not prevail against the church (Matthew 16:18).
- The Law was read to the people there.

REVIVAL—NEHEMIAH 8–13:3

In the rebuilding of the city walls, Nehemiah organized well and fought off all of the satanic opposition. The Word of God was central to the project and was read to the people for six straight hours. The people committed to obey God. The project was completed in an astonishing fifty-two days! The people confessed their sins and covenanted with God once again. Ezra and Nehemiah dedicated the walls after a great procession.

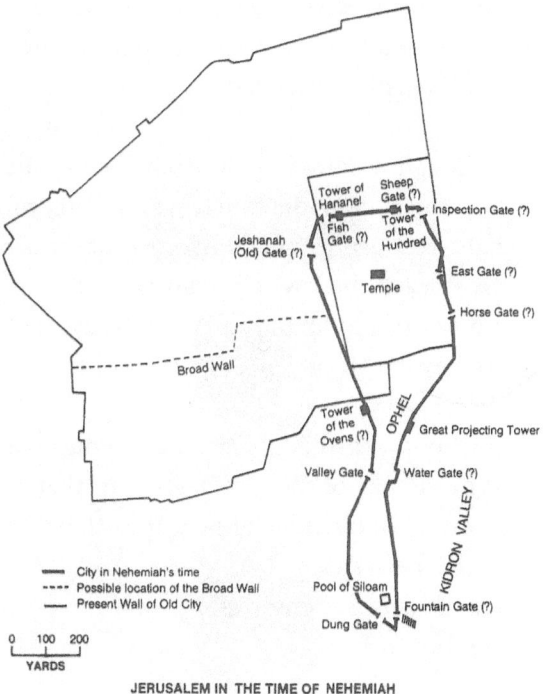

JERUSALEM IN THE TIME OF NEHEMIAH

REPAIRING SPIRITUAL LEAKS—NEHEMIAH 13:4–31

The last chapter brought the people back to their spiritual roots, as Nehemiah used some harsh tactics to reinforce his message.

Esther
The Book of Faith

OUTLINE
1. Danger (1–4)
2. Deliverance (5–10)

INTRODUCTION
The book of Esther in many ways has been one of the most puzzling books in all of Scripture. There are two books in the Word of God named after a woman. Ruth is the story of a Gentile who married a Jew. Esther is the story of a Jewess who married a Gentile.

Although it comes in order of books after Nehemiah, its events antedate Nehemiah by about thirty years. This probably occurred during a fifty-eight-year gap in the book of Ezra between chapters 6 and 7. This, then, is the story of the Jews who did not return to Jerusalem, but chose rather the prosperity and luxury of Persia. They were out of God's will, but they were not beyond His care.

The book of Esther is part of the group called the Antilegomena. It consists of five books of the Old Testament that were disputed as to whether they belonged in the Bible or not. The other four besides Esther are:
1. Ecclesiastes
2. Song of Solomon
3. Proverbs
4. Ezekiel

The charges against the five are as follows:
1. Ecclesiastes: It is fatalistic and says life is meaningless. There is much doom and despair, yet without God that's how life is.

2. Song of Solomon: Too sensual; physical love is detailed here, yet within marriage God is pleased with it.
3. Proverbs: Appears to be a contradiction in 26:4–5—don't answer a fool/answer a fool. Yet, this is talking about two different situations.
4. Ezekiel: Is supposedly anti-Mosaic, yet looks forward to the millennial kingdom—not to the law.
5. Esther: The name of God is not mentioned—it is the only book in the Bible without God's name; however, God is shown all over through His sovereignty.

Esther also has two other oddities about it:
1. It is never quoted in the New Testament.
2. It never mentions prayer and Old Testament rituals.

But this is a wonderful truth about God—even though we at times do not acknowledge His presence, He is at work in His people. Matthew Henry, in his devotional commentary, said this: *"Though the name of God be not in it, the finger of God is."*[15]

FAST FACTS
- The authorship is uncertain, but likely Ezra. It was written about 470 BC.
- This is the book of Salvation to the Jews. It is placed right next to the Pentateuch in the Hebrew Bible.
- Esther means "star."
- The overall theme is "the providence of God" (see Romans 8:28).
- The purpose appears to be threefold:
    1. To show God's providential care
    2. To explain the Feast of Purim
    3. To show what happened to the Jews who did not return to Israel after the Babylonian captivity

INTERESTING NOTE:
Anti-Semitism is as old as the history of Israel itself. Over the centuries this tiny nation has endured cruel hatred, captivity, and injustice. The capital city

of Jerusalem has been leveled seventeen times, only to have it rebuilt again. Two things stand out in God's dealings with Israel:
1. The nations who opposed Israel brought about their own downfall.
2. Attempting to annihilate Israel through a pogrom (a systematic killing of a people group) only resulted in Israel being blessed.

God promised to "bless" Israel in the Abrahamic covenant of Genesis 12, and this was regardless of all the other nations.

DANGER—ESTHER 1-4

Xerxes was an interesting Persian king. He was a neurotic ruler who was king during Esther's time. He thought of himself as a god. In chapter 1, Xerxes threw a party for seven days and an open house for 180 days. The affair ended with the ousting of the queen of Persia. Esther took her place.

Xerxes was a king about to lose his dominating empire. Daniel the prophet had predicted in chapter 2 of his own book that the Medo-Persian Empire would fall and that the Greeks would succeed them. This was beginning to happen in Xerxes' day, so he turned to pleasure.

During this time, Haman, a trusted official in the king's court, plotted to destroy all Jews because Mordecai, who had raised Esther, refused to honor Haman. Esther was sovereignly placed into her position of power "for such a time as this" (4:14), yet she feared getting involved. Mordecai convinced her otherwise.

DELIVERANCE—ESTHER 5-10

Haman's plan backfired, and the gallows he had prepared for Mordecai were now used to end his life. Ironically, the king then elevated the Jewish Mordecai to a high-level government position. Anti-Semitism was wiped out in Persia for a time. The book is a picture of the sovereignty of God. God controls all things even if from behind the scenes. Nowhere can this be seen any better than in the book of Esther, where God's name is not mentioned, yet He is in reality the central character of the book. The Feast of the Purim is still celebrated today by Jews as a remembrance of God's delivery during Esther's days.

OLD TESTAMENT

Job

The Book of Enduring Faith

OUTLINE
1. Distress (1–2:10)
2. Discussion (2:11–37)
3. Deliverance (38–42)

INTRODUCTION

We have now covered the seventeen Historical Books, which make up the first part of the Old Testament, from Genesis to Esther. Next is a smaller and very different group of books—the five Poetic Books. These books are composed almost entirely of Hebrew verse. The style of the content is poetic, but that does not mean that this section of Scripture is in any way fictitious or imaginative.

Spiritual Progress in the Poetic Books:
1. Job: Death of self
2. Psalms: New life in God
3. Proverbs: Practical wisdom for life
4. Ecclesiastes: Warning of earthly things and their futility
5. Song of Solomon: Love

Comparisons	
Historical Books	**Poetic Books**
Stress facts	Stress personal experience
Emphasize the nation of Israel	Emphasize the individual
Highlight the Hebrew race	Highlight the human heart

Length of Sections	
Historical Section	249 Chapters
Poetic Section	243 Chapters
Prophetic Section	250 Chapters

Problems Presented in the Poetic Books:
1. Job: Why do the righteous suffer?
2. Psalms: How do we worship?
3. Proverbs: How do I live?
4. Ecclesiastes: What is the meaning of life?
5. Song of Solomon: What is the meaning of love between husband and wife?

In the opinion of many, the book of Job is the most remarkable book in the entire Bible:

Lord Tennyson: "*The greatest poem, whether of ancient or modern literature.*"[16]
Martin Luther: "*This book is magnificent and sublime as no other book of Scripture.*"[17]
Thomas Carlyle: "*I call [this book], apart from all theories about it, one of the grandest things ever written . . . There is nothing written, I think, . . . of equal literary merit.*"[18]
Philip Schaff: "*It rises like a pyramid in the history of literature, without a predecessor and without a rival.*"[19]

The book of Job is actually a philosophic discussion, in highly poetic language, of the problem of human suffering. How could a good God make a world filled with so many inequalities and injustices? The book does not solve the whole problem of human suffering, but it helps in the understanding of the problem.

Job Raises Five Important Questions:
1. Is goodness rewarded?
   Yes, here or in heaven.
2. Why do the righteous suffer and the sinful don't?
   Not necessarily so.
3. Does God care about and protect His people?
   Yes.
4. Is suffering always a sign of sin?
   No.
5. Does God have mercy for all?
   Yes.

In the discussion that Job had with his friends, the answers he was given were according to the common philosophy of that day. Job had at one time accepted these answers but now was groping for the truth.

FAST FACTS
- The author is unknown. Job, Moses, and Samuel are suggested.
- Job means "one who turns back."
- Job is probably the oldest book in the Bible. The date of writing is unclear.
- The reason it's believed to be the oldest book is that there is not one mention of the Law or the miracles in the history of Israel.
- The theme is "Why do the righteous suffer?"

DISTRESS—JOB 1:1–2:10
Job is described as being "blameless" in the first chapter of the book. He was not perfect, but he could not be accused of any overt sins. He sacrificed burnt offerings for himself and his family. Satan approached God and accused Job of serving God merely because of all the good in his life. God gave Satan permission to test Job. Satan in the presence of God proves:
- He is accountable to God.
- He is allowed by God to roam.
- Satan is behind evil.

- Satin is limited in wisdom and in locale. He is not omniscient (does not know all things) or omnipresent (cannot be in all places at once), as God is.

Job lost everything. His suffering was intense. He lost ten children, all of his livestock, and his workers. He lost his health also. Job's wife assumed God was judging Job. He rejected this.

DISCUSSION—JOB: 2:11-37

Job was silent for seven days, and so were his friends. His three friends, Eliphaz, Bildad, and Zophar all tried to counsel Job. They were failures at comforting him. By chapter 3, Job wanted to give up and die. At this point, it was hard to blame him. Instead of bringing Job encouragement, his friends debated him. In the end, Job's friends heaped guilt on him because of what they perceived as a hidden sin in his life.

DELIVERANCE—JOB 38-42

God came to Job's rescue. He began with dozens of questions for Job. Job was unable to answer even one of them since they had to do with the wisdom of God. They also had to do with how God created the earth. Job finally answered God in 40:4-5. "I am unworthy—how can I reply to you? I put my hand over my mouth . . . I will say no more." This was the point at which God wanted Job to arrive—broken and with no answers. Then God stepped in and prospered Job again. He gave him twice as much as he'd ever had before. The Lord blessed Job's later life more than He had his earlier life. Job is the portrait of trials in the Bible.

Psalms

The Book of Worship

OUTLINE
1. Section 1 (1–41)
2. Section 2 (42–72)
3. Section 3 (73–89)
4. Section 4 (90–106)
5. Section 5 (107–150)

INTRODUCTION

The book of Psalms is the heart of the Bible. It begins with God blessing man (Psalm 1) and ends with man blessing God (Psalm 150). In between, we find every type of human experience as seen in the light of eternity. The Psalms are truly the "heart throb" of the Bible. Psalms stir the emotions. J. Sidlow Baxter said, *"Psalms is a limpid lake which reflects every mood of man's changeful sky."*[20]

FAST FACTS

- Fifty Psalms are called "orphan psalms" since their authorship is unknown. The remaining one hundred psalms were written by the following seven writers:
    › David—seventy-three psalms
    › Asaph—twelve psalms
    › Sons of Korah—ten psalms
    › Heman—one psalm
    › Ethan—one psalm
    › Solomon—two psalms
    › Moses—one psalm
- Psalms is quoted in the New Testament more than all other thirty-eight Old Testament books combined.

- The chapters of the Psalms were written over a period of one thousand years, from 1440 to 586 BC.
- The title "Psalms" can be translated "the Book of Praise Psalms."

They Were Written Under Various Passions:
1. Penitence (sorrow over sin): Psalms 6, 32, 51, 88
2. Praise: Psalms 30, 40, 103, 107, 144, 150
3. Prayer: Psalms 13, 25, 28, 55, 141, 143
4. Provocation (when agitated or upset): Psalms 35, 52, 57, 69, 137
5. Patriotism (the presence of the Lord in Israel and His mighty works in Israel): Psalm 114

They Were Written for Various Purposes:
1. Victory celebrations
2. Laying of the foundation of the temple
3. The pilgrimage of the Jews to Jerusalem
4. Songs for various feasts
5. Prophetic, especially messianic

The Psalms can be classified into some general categories. They are:
1. Nature psalms: describing God's works and wonders (Psalm 8)
2. Righteous psalms: describing righteous man (Psalm 7)
3. Historical psalms: epic poems/hero poems (Psalm 33)
4. Penitential psalms: expressing sorrow for sin (Psalm 51)
5. Imprecatory psalms: a call for God to destroy enemies (Psalm 35)
6. Theocratic psalms: to set forth the characteristics of God (Psalm 90)
7. Hallel psalms (praise): Passover night (Psalm 113, 114, before meals; 115–118 after)
8. Pilgrim psalms: these were sung by those making a pilgrimage to Jerusalem for the feasts of Passover, Pentecost, and Tabernacles (Psalm 120–134)
9. Hallelujah psalms: each begins and ends with "Hallelujah" or "Praise the Lord" (Psalm 146)
10. Messianic psalms: the ultimate explanation found in Christ (Psalm 22)

SECTION 1—PSALMS 1–41
The book of Psalms gives us the thoughts and feelings of Israelites living out their faith. It is an invaluable source of devotional material that appeals to the heart. It is like medicine for the soul. It is the sourcebook for thousands of hymns and praise songs. No other book of the Bible has such a strong connection to music. Psalm 1 opens aptly with a contrast of the righteous man and the wicked man. Psalm 23 has brought more comfort to the hurting than perhaps any other chapter of the entire Bible.

SECTION 2—PSALMS 42–72
King David's famous confession of his sin with Bathsheba is detailed in chapter 51. This is a textbook on asking the Lord for forgiveness. Psalm 63 answers the question, "How can I have peace in my life?" The answer is found in seeking God with our whole hearts.

SECTION 3—PSALMS 73–89
Psalm 77 provides God's remedy for a big problem. Asaph was overwhelmed by his problems yet remembers God's power and miracles and is victorious over it all.

SECTION 4—PSALMS 90–106
Psalm 93 inspires us as the writer lifts us to the throne of God in all of its majesty. Psalm 98 is messianic in nature as it prophesies the Anointed One's ministry. Jesus fulfilled these verses, as He came to save all people from their sins.

SECTION 5—PSALMS 107–150
Psalm 119 describes the Word of God in all its glory. It is written as an acrostic. There are twenty-two sections—one for each letter of the Hebrew alphabet. Each section contains eight verses. The Word of God contains ten synonyms used numerous times in Psalm 119. They are:
1. Law: 25 times
2. Word: 20 times
3. Saying: 9 times

4. Commandments: 21 times
5. Statutes: 21 times
6. Judgment: 19 times
7. Precept: 21 times
8. Testimony: 22 times
9. Way: 5 times
10. Path: 5 times

Above all, this tells us how to live a pure, pleasing life before God.

Psalms 140–150 joyously praise our wonderful God.

Proverbs
The Book of Wise Living

> **OUTLINE**
> 1. Sermons for Sons (1–10)
> 2. Messages for Mankind (11–20)
> 3. Lessons for Leaders (21–31)

INTRODUCTION

A proverb is a precept or a saying that governs our conduct in life. Proverbs are in many ways shortened parables. Proverbs comprises a library of moral and spiritual instruction to ensure a godly life, the rewards for which are in part received here but fully compensated in heaven.

Just as Psalms is directed toward our devotional life, Proverbs is directed toward our practical life. Psalms is written to make our hearts warm toward God, while Proverbs makes our faces shine before men with the example of righteous living. In Psalms, the love of God is shown; in Proverbs the love of people is shown.

FAST FACTS

- The date of writing is from 950 to 700 BC, and the book was written largely by Solomon.
- Proverbs means "wise sayings."
- A proverb is defined as "a short sentence conveying moral truth in a concise and pointed form."[21] Solomon wrote more than three thousand proverbs, yet he was guided by the Spirit of God to write several hundred included in the book of Proverbs. Agur wrote the thirtieth chapter, and his background is unknown. Lemuel wrote chapter 31. Although he is listed as a king, little is known about him.
- Important subjects: wisdom, righteousness, fear of god, morality, diligence, self-control, giving/saving, choosing friends, raising children, honesty.

WORDS AND SPEAKING IN PROVERBS

Wrong Uses of Words:
- Lying: Proverbs 6:16–17a; 10:18a; 12:19, 22a; 17:4b, 7; 19:5b, 9b, 22b; 21:6; 26:28a
- Slandering: Proverbs 10:18b; 30:10
- Gossiping: Proverbs 11:13; 16:28b; 17:9b; 18:8; 20:19; 26:20, 22
- Constant talking: Proverbs 10:8, 10b,19; 17:28; 18:2; 20:19b
- False witnessing: Proverbs 12:17b; 14:5b, 25b; 19:5a, 28a; 21:28; 25:18
- Mocking: Proverbs 13:1b; 14:6a; 15:12; 17:5a; 19:29a; 21:11a; 22:10; 24:9b; 30:17
- Harsh talking (perverse, reckless, harsh, evil, sly words): Proverbs 10:31b–32; 12:18a; 13:3b; 14:3a; 15:1b, 28b; 17:4a; 19:1, 28b
- Boasting: Proverbs 17:17a; 20:14; 25:14; 27:1–2
- Quarreling: Proverbs 13:10; 15:18; 17:14, 19; 19:13; 20:3; 21:9, 19; 22:10; 25:24; 26:17, 20–21; 27:15
- Deceiving: Proverbs 7:19–20; 12:2; 15:4b; 25:23
- Flattering: Proverbs 26:28b; 28:23; 29:5
- Ignorant or foolish words: Proverbs 14:7; 15:2b, 7–14; 18:6–7

Right Uses of Words:
- Words that help and encourage: Proverbs 10:11a, 20a, 21a; 12:14a, 18b; 15:4a; 18:4, 20–21
- Words that express wisdom: Proverbs 10:13a, 31a; 14:3b; 15:2a, 7a; 16:10, 21b, 23b; 20:15
- Words that are few: Proverbs 10:19; 11:12b; 13:3a; 17:27a
- Words that are fitting (kind, appropriate, pleasant): Proverbs 10:32a; 12:25; 15:1a, 4a, 23; 16:24; 25:11, 15
- Words that are true: Proverbs 12:17a, 19a, 22b; 14:5a, 25a
- Words that are carefully chosen: Proverbs 13:3a; 15:28; 16:23a; 21:23

Why do we sin with our mouths (Proverbs 10:19)? Because we talk! The tongue is the only muscle that gains strength with usage rather than growing tired! Talking has to be curbed to avoid it! It's so natural for us.

SERMONS FOR SONS—PROVERBS 1–10

Wisdom is acquired, and it comes from years of discipline. It begins with the Lord: "The fear of the LORD is the beginning of knowledge, but fools despise wisdom and instruction," or discipline (Proverbs 1:7). Discipline and wisdom go hand in hand. Proverbs 5 details how people fall into immorality.

MESSAGES FOR MANKIND—PROVERBS 11–20

The key word in this section is righteousness or right living. Proverbs 14:34 is God's view of the world. It simply states, "Righteousness exalts a nation, but sin condemns any people."

LESSONS FOR LEADERS—PROVERBS 21–31

Proverbs 21:1 states that the king's heart is in the hand of God. Despite free will, God uses all world rulers however he wishes. Proverbs 31 is about a woman who over the scope of her life accomplished much to the glory of God.

Ecclesiastes
The Book of Human Reason

OUTLINE
1. "Does Life Have Meaning?" (1:1–11)
2. "Life Is Confusing" (1:12–11:6)
3. Conclusions (11:7–12:14)

INTRODUCTION

Ecclesiastes is a favorite book of atheists, agnostics, and cultists. From Voltaire, the French skeptic, to the Jehovah's Witnesses, the book has been used to prove almost anything. Therefore, it is of utmost importance to understand the purpose and meaning of the book.

Ecclesiastes is the book of the natural man, which details his reasonings and actions apart from divine revelation. A New Testament explanation of this is found in 1 Corinthians 2:14. The phrase "under the sun" is found in the book some thirty times. The writer looked at life through creation and not divine revelations. This is so important to understand because man cannot fully come to God, understand Him, and enjoy Him through creation alone. Without God revealing Himself to us through divine revelation, man is stumped in his search for God. Not only that, but without divine perspective, life appears to be useless in and of itself. The word for God in Ecclesiastes is *Elohim*—"Creator." The word Jehovah—"Lord"—is not used. God uses this book to demonstrate how "bankrupt" human philosophy is apart from this divine revelation. Thus, since the writer is recounting his journey through life, minus the influence of a personal relationship with God, the preliminary conclusions are contrary to Scripture.

FAST FACTS

- The author is probably Solomon. Intellectually brilliant, yet apart from God, he could not understand God or life! The book was written

around 935 BC.
- Ecclesiastes is the Latin word for "preacher."
- The theme is "Life is futile without God." The phrase "under the sun" is used thirty times; "all is vanity" appears thirty-seven times, depending on the translation one reads. The NIV translates this heart cry as "Meaningless!"
- The final word: God is good; God is wise; God is just. Therefore, enjoy life with Him!

"DOES LIFE HAVE MEANING?"—ECCLESIASTES 1:1–11

Solomon wrote Ecclesiastes as if he were speaking to a group of people. His conclusions were that life is meaningless and monotonous.

"LIFE IS CONFUSING"—ECCLESIASTES 1:12–11:6

Solomon looked at life through human achievement. He was the smartest man of his day and accomplished much for God, yet it left him unfulfilled. He next turned to pleasure, wealth, and materialism; and they too left him feeling empty.

CONCLUSIONS—ECCLESIASTES 11:7–12:14

Solomon concluded that life without God is not worth living. He called his audience to "fear God and keep his commandments" (12:13). This is what's most important in life.

Song of Solomon
The Book of Love

> **OUTLINE**
> 1. The Courting (1–3:5)
> 2. The Wedding (3:6–11)
> 3. The Marriage (4–5:1)
> 4. The Conflict (5:2–6:13)
> 5. The Commitment (7–8:4)
> 6. The Conclusion (8:5–14)

INTRODUCTION

The Song of Solomon is a poem that consists of several speeches. It is a book about love; and since it is graphic in nature, not too many sermons are preached from it. For centuries, Jews would not permit men under thirty years old to even read it. It was often called the "Holy of Holies of Scripture."

FAST FACTS

- Solomon is the author of this Book of Love.
- The title is the "Song of Songs."
- It was written around 965 BC.
- The theme is "the permanence of true love."
- The book covers Solomon's love relationship with his Shulammite bride—their courtship, wedding, honeymoon, first conflict, reunion, and finally, the maturity of their love.

THE COURTING—SONG OF SOLOMON 1–3:5

The author depicted the love attraction that the bride has for Solomon, and he for her. Observing were the daughters of Jerusalem as the lovers verbalized their hopes and dreams. Solomon used this section to portray his and his bride's deep affection and desire for each other. Obviously, there is no question that they were seriously in love and wanting to marry.

THE WEDDING—SONG OF SOLOMON 3:6-11
Solomon's desire to protect and provide for his wife is seen here.

THE MARRIAGE—SONG OF SOLOMON 4-5:1
The honeymoon is described in detail as the two lovers drink of the wine of love. The verbal exchange is seen as they tell of their love and commitment to one another. Picturesque language was the vehicle used to dramatize the scene—the glorious celebration of their consummation.

THE CONFLICT—SONG OF SOLOMON 5:2-6:13
The first marital fight is not what is stressed in this section. But what the author intended here is to show the readers and the daughters of Jerusalem how the lovers handle their quarrel with maturity. The bride's confidence is apparent, as she knows her lover will be off at his favorite garden. One fight could not undo their love.

THE COMMITMENT—SONG OF SOLOMON 7-8:4
In this reunion section, the two relive their honeymoon with love poems again to each other. Solomon looks upon the maturity they have developed and admonishes the daughters of Jerusalem to wait for love and not "awaken" it until it so desires (8:4). Their kind of love commitment would be found if they didn't hurry love!

THE CONCLUSION—SONG OF SOLOMON 8:5-14
Solomon and his wife's reminiscing provides a closing glimpse at their journey of romance. With final encouragement to the people in the art of marriage, the author closes the curtain. As the book ends, the continual love relationship is seen one more time as the two again exchange love back and forth verbally. The daughters of Jerusalem and readers alike today are provided with a biblical painting of true love, which has all the God-ordained ingredients:
- Desire for each other
- Maturity
- Contentment
- Happiness

Isaiah
The Book of Salvation

> **OUTLINE**
> Prophecies of Condemnation (1–35)
> The History of the Times (36–39)
> Prophecies of Consolation (40–66)

INTRODUCTION

Isaiah is the prophet of prophets. His 66-chapter book begins the section of the Bible aptly called the Major Prophets. Since the book is so messianic in nature, it has been called the Fifth Gospel. The section after the Major Prophets is the Minor Prophets. It consists of twelve books, yet Isaiah has more words than all of the Minor Prophets combined. He is the chief writing prophet and is mentioned eighty times in the New Testament. Also, twenty of the twenty-seven New Testament books quote Isaiah.

FAST FACTS

- Isaiah is the author, and the book was written over twenty years, between 700 and 681 BC.
- Isaiah means "Jehovah saves."
- His ministry was primarily to the southern kingdom of Judah.
- His ministry also spanned five kings and a total of sixty to sixty-five years.
- Tradition tells us that Isaiah was martyred by King Manasseh. He was placed in a hollow log and sawn in half.
- Isaiah's character is most noteworthy. He possessed:
  - great boldness
  - great earnestness
  - an uncompromising attitude toward sin
  - tenderness and compassion

- The Prophetic Books deal with three major themes:
  - the Messiah
  - the Kingdom of God
  - the Day of the Lord
- Isaiah speaks about all three of these.
- Isaiah was also able to see the conditions that led to the nation's spiritual decline. They were more concerned with outward, formal ceremonies than true, inward, spiritual transformation.
- Isaiah is emotional and at the same time a literary genius.

PROPHECIES OF CONDEMNATION—ISAIAH 1–35

The first chapter lays before the people the case against Israel. Isaiah gets straight to the point—even dumb animals know their master, but the people do not know theirs (see 1:3). Their worship was unacceptable, as God says they spread their hands out in prayer, but He hides His eyes from them. For Israel, ritualism had replaced passion for God. The feast, ceremonies, and laws were duties to them—their participation was not heartfelt. God said that Jerusalem had become a harlot.

God urged repentance and offered forgiveness to the people. It was still not too late!

> "Come now, let us reason together, says the Lord: though your sins are like scarlet, they shall be as white as snow." (1:18 RSV)

In the midst of God's indictment of the people, Isaiah 6 is a beacon of light in the midst of the spiritual darkness. Isaiah sees a picture of God's holiness and is struck hard by his own sinfulness.

> In the year that King Uzziah died, I saw the Lord, high and exalted, seated on a throne; and the train of his robe filled the temple. Above him were seraphim, each with six wings: With two wings they covered their faces, with two they covered their feet, and with two they were flying. And they were calling to one another:

"Holy, holy, holy is the Lord Almighty;
   the whole earth is full of his glory."
At the sound of their voices the doorposts and thresholds shook and the temple was filled with smoke.

"Woe to me!" I cried. "I am ruined! For I am a man of unclean lips, and I live among a people of unclean lips, and my eyes have seen the King, the Lord Almighty."

Then one of the seraphim flew to me with a live coal in his hand, which he had taken with tongs from the altar. With it he touched my mouth and said, "See, this has touched your lips; your guilt is taken away and your sin atoned for."

Then I heard the voice of the Lord saying, "Whom shall I send? And who will go for us?"

And I said, "Here am I. Send me!"

He said, "Go and tell this people:
"'Be ever hearing, but never understanding;
   be ever seeing, but never perceiving.'
Make the heart of this people calloused;
   make their ears dull
   and close their eyes.
Otherwise they might see with their eyes,
   hear with their ears,
   understand with their hearts,
and turn and be healed."
Then I said, "For how long, Lord?"

And he answered:
"Until the cities lie ruined
   and without inhabitant,
until the houses are left deserted

and the fields ruined and ravaged,
until the Lord has sent everyone far away
   and the land is utterly forsaken.
And though a tenth remains in the land,
   it will again be laid waste.
But as the terebinth and oak
   leave stumps when they are cut down,
   so the holy seed will be the stump in the land."
(Isaiah 6)

The glory of the Lord overwhelmed Isaiah, and he was willing to go to the obstinate people as God's spokesman. God tells him that his ministry would be until the cities were leveled and the people were captured. God's holiness demanded a harsh message to the sinful people.

Isaiah 9 predicted the coming of the Messiah from the line of David. "The Way of the Sea" is the road that the Romans would build seven hundred years after Isaiah was written. Their highway, which went along the northern part of the Sea of Galilee, was called the "Via Maris," which means "the way of the sea." The Messiah's reign would be a wonderful one of righteousness and justice, as He is the Prince of Peace.

THE HISTORY OF THE TIMES—ISAIAH 36–39

The events of these chapters are from Hezekiah's reign. Two great miracles occurred here:
1. The Angel of the Lord destroyed the Assyrian army that was ready to invade Jerusalem. There were 185,000 soldiers killed.
2. Hezekiah was dying, and God answered the king's prayer and gave him fifteen more years of life. (Isa. 38:5)

PROPHECIES OF CONSOLATION—ISAIAH 40–66

Chapters 1–39 are the "Old Testament" of Isaiah. The twenty-seven remaining chapters, 40–66, are the "New Testament" of Isaiah. Interestingly, the Old Testament does in fact have thirty-nine books and the New Testament twenty-seven!

Chapter 40 begins with the plan of the ages being unrolled as John the Baptist heralds the arrival of the Messiah. God's kingdom authority is seen in the coming Holy One of Israel, who will restore all things to God.

Isaiah 53 is perhaps the premier passage of Jesus Christ as the Messiah in all of the Old Testament. The prophetical details are all fulfilled in Jesus of Nazareth.

Chapter 66 talks about the regathering of the nation of Israel.

Jeremiah

The Book of Warning

OUTLINE
1. Jeremiah's Call (1)
2. Judah's Fate (2–39)
3. After the Fall (40–45)
4. Prophecies to the Nations (46–52)

INTRODUCTION

Jeremiah's message to Judah and other nations was one of impending doom. God gave Judah chances to amend their ways, but they didn't. The intent of Jeremiah was for Judah to repent, as he preached the same message over and over for years. God gave him several illustrations to use in the messages to graphically portray Judah's fate. Jeremiah wept his way through his messages as his heart broke over and over for his disobedient nation.

Jeremiah states that people had sinned and remain aloof from God, and God would specifically judge them. In order to bring submission to God's discipline (captivity), Jeremiah traced their sins and chances to repent throughout the book—they would not repent; therefore, God sent devastation and judgment.

Jeremiah represented God's final effort to save Jerusalem. Jeremiah lived about 125 years after Isaiah. Isaiah had seen Jerusalem saved from the Assyrians. Jeremiah tried to save the city from the Babylonians but failed.

Jeremiah lived through the last forty agonizing years; and before Israel's captivity, witnessed the death of his beloved nation. He witnessed three stages:
1. Jerusalem partially destroyed—605 BC.
2. Jerusalem laid waste—597 BC.
3. Jerusalem buried and evacuated—587 BC.

FAST FACTS
- Jeremiah wrote the book between 627 and 586 BC.
- The title means, "whom Jehovah establishes."
- His father was a priest.
- Anathoth was his city, of the tribe of Benjamin.
- He was chosen before birth to lead.
- He started preaching when he was young.
- He preached during the lives of five kings of Judah.
- He faced more persecution and rejection than just about anyone.
- His message was a stern warning against the doom of Babylonian captivity if they didn't repent.
- There is not much said about the future but hellfire and brimstone!
- Jeremiah's confessions are:
  › tremendously tense
  › very emotional
  › sensitive

Yet, he was ordered to preach boldly.

JEREMIAH'S CALL—JEREMIAH 1

The call of Jeremiah before his birth set the stage for his life of ministry ahead. In 1:5, God says that He "knew" Jeremiah before his birth. The Hebrew word *yada* is used here, and it means far more than intellectual knowledge. It is used of an intimate relationship that is very personal. There were no options for Jeremiah. He made no excuses, unlike Moses and Jonah at their commissioning. In fact, God warned Jeremiah not to use for an excuse his youthful age (v. 7).

God begins with two visions:
1. The almond branch
2. The boiling pot

The almond branch signified that God was watching Israel as the almond tree hovers over them, giving shade. The almond tree blooms first of all the trees in Israel, thus meaning God's judgment would be swift.

The boiling pot was poured from the north to south, signifying that judgment was coming from the north, namely the Babylonians.

JUDAH'S FATE—JEREMIAH 2-39

This section enumerates ten messages that concern Judah and all of its inhabitants. In one of the messages, Jeremiah breaks a clay pot that cannot be put back together. So would be the fate of Israel if they did not repent. A special section was written to address the problem of false prophets. In chapter 26, Jeremiah was put on trial and threatened with death. In chapter 32, the glorious words of the new covenant are laid out. God would make a new covenant with the house of Israel. This covenant would put the law of God on their hearts. Chapter 39 records the fall of Jerusalem.

AFTER THE FALL—JEREMIAH 40-45

Chaos reigns after the Babylonian invasion. Jeremiah was captured and taken to Egypt against his will.

PROPHECIES—JEREMIAH 46-52

Chapters 46-51 list the coming fury of God to no fewer than ten Gentile nations. In detail, the fall of Jerusalem concludes the book as Israel is taken off to captivity in Babylon. Jeremiah has been called the weeping prophet. He had a sad, lonely life and was forbidden to marry. He had no converts or followers, as no one listened to him. He also watched in horror as the temple of the Lord was destroyed systematically by Nebuchadnezzar's army.

In all of his sadness, he remained faithful to God.

Lamentations
The Book of Sorrow

> OUTLINE
> 1. Result of Israel's Sin (1)
> 2. God's Judgment (2)
> 3. Hope (3–4)
> 4. Jeremiah Pleads for Jerusalem (5)

INTRODUCTION

The book of Lamentations is perhaps the saddest book of the Bible. It is the epilogue to Jeremiah, and tradition teaches us that the prophet wrote it on Golgotha, the very place where our Savior would give His life for our sins.

FAST FACTS

- It is clear that Jeremiah wrote it to illustrate the consequences of sin. It was written shortly after the fall of Jerusalem in 586 BC.
- The title means "an expression of grief or sorrow."
- The book is written in poetic form as an acrostic, which is an alphabetic progression through all twenty-two Hebrew letters.

THE RESULTS OF ISRAEL'S SINS—LAMENTATIONS 1

Jeremiah described the devastation of the city of Jerusalem. Jerusalem is represented here as a woman speaking for herself. She confesses her sin and repents.

GOD'S JUDGMENT—LAMENTATIONS 2

Zion is a synonym for Jerusalem, and God called the daughters of Zion the recipients of His wrath. He eventually ruined Zion, and the devastation was merely a fulfillment of His repeated warnings as stated in verse 17.

HOPE—LAMENTATIONS 3-4

This is a beautiful portion of scripture highlighted by the verse that says, "For His compassions never fail. They are new every morning; great is your faithfulness" (3:22–23).

JEREMIAH PLEADS FOR JERUSALEM—LAMENTATIONS 5

Jeremiah cried out in anguish for his beloved Jerusalem. Exodus 3:7 tells us the Lord is concerned when His people suffer. The fall of Jerusalem is the saddest of moments for our living God. The temple was gone. The people were in bondage and removed from the land. It is much like the time when Israel was bound in slavery in Egypt.

Ezekiel
The Book of Glory

OUTLINE
1. The Condemnation of Judah (1–24)
2. The Condemnation of Gentiles (25–32)
3. The Restoration (33–48)

INTRODUCTION
Among the writing prophets, Ezekiel stands out for his mystical and mystifying visions, his symbolic enactment of his prophecies, his emphatic repetitions, and his furious oratory. He reminds us of Jeremiah in his preaching and object lessons, but not in his personality.

To the average reader, the book appears like a kaleidoscope that defies interpretation. The book is filled with the glory of God. Ezekiel has been called the prophet of the glory of God. He saw:
- the Lord's glory at his commissioning (chapter 1)
- the Shekinah glory leaving the temple (chapter 10)
- the glory of the future kingdom (chapters 40-48

FAST FACTS
- Ezekiel wrote the book around 570 BC.
- Ezekiel was a twenty-five-year-old captive in Babylonian refugee camps.
- Ezekiel was the son of a priest and owned a home.
- He used many methods, including symbols, visions, parables, and poems, to get attention.
- Ezekiel wanted to show that God was justified in sending Israel into captivity.
- The "glory of God" is mentioned nineteen times.
- The key phrase, which is translated in some versions "they shall know that I am the LORD," is used sixty times!

THE CONDEMNATION OF JUDAH—EZEKIEL 1-24

Ezekiel wrote during dark days for Israel. As a refugee in Babylon, he saw beyond their present sufferings and to the coming glory of God. In chapter 1, Ezekiel viewed a spectacular sight as the hand of the Lord came upon him. He viewed up close the glory of God. When he saw it, he was overwhelmed and fell facedown before the Lord.

The angels in Ezekiel are given names and a classification in Scripture.

NAMES
Angels—Messengers
Chariots—Army of God
Ministers—Servants
Watchers—Supervisors
Host—Army of God

CLASSIFICATION:
Cherubim: The highest order of angels—indescribable powers and beauty—character and appearance far beyond human imagination—"proclaimers" and "protectors" of God's glorious presence. They are always in God's presence. Cherubim are seen also in Genesis in the garden of Eden.

Seraphim: "The burning ones." They are consumed with devotion to God. Seraphim performed a priest's duty before God, specifically, adoration and praise of holy God.

Living Creatures: They are the worshippers of God. Also they are seen in Scripture as directing the judgments of God.

ARCHANGELS
Michael: Michael is God's military leader, created in the class of cherubim. Michael holds a high rank among the angelic beings.
Duties: As in Daniel's day, he wages great warfare with Satan. Also, he is a defender of Israel.

Gabriel: His name means "Mighty One of God." He possesses unusual speed and great power. He is God's Messenger. He appears four times in Scripture: he announced John the Baptist's birth, he announced Jesus' birth, he announced the seventy weeks prophecy in Daniel 9, and he announced the Antichrist in Daniel 8.

The sadness of this section is seen as the glory of the Lord leaves the temple through the eastern gate (chapter 10). Ezekiel used dramatic signs to get the people's attention to warn of this awful time in their history, but to no avail.

THE CONDEMNATION OF GENTILES—EZEKIEL 25-32

Ezekiel predicted the judgments on the Gentiles during the siege on Jerusalem. God lists seven of Israel's worst enemies of all time:
1. Ammon
2. Moab
3. Edom
4. Philistia
5. Tyre
6. Sidon
7. Egypt

Seven is the number for God in the Bible, and God would judge Israel's seven worst enemies in the midst of their coming captivity. God would not allow their enemies to gloat.

THE RESTORATION—EZEKIEL 33-48

The predictions in this section are made after the siege of Jerusalem. This section contains two extremely important promises. In chapter 34, the Messiah as the true Shepherd of Israel is prophesied. He would be a prince among His people. In chapters 36 and 37, the spectacular restoration of the nation of Israel is laid out. God said in 36:24 that He would take Israel out of the nations and bring them back to their land. This miracle happened May 14, 1948, as Israel became a nation again after 1,882 years of displacement from their land.

Daniel
The Book of the Apocalypse

OUTLINE
1. The Historical Section (1–6)
2. The Prophetic Section (7–12)

INTRODUCTION

Daniel is known mainly for his unwavering life and incredible miracles, at first glance. But the book of Daniel is primarily an apocalyptic book. This word *apocalyptic* means "to unveil or make known."

Apocalyptic literature has several characteristics.
- It is revealed through visions.
- It makes extensive use of symbols or signs.
- It is about Israel and the future.
- A time line is established through the sum of all biblical writings.

Interpreting visions, signs, and symbols in the Bible is done with consistent methods by:
- examining the content
- comparing the passage with parallel passages.

FAST FACTS
- The book of Daniel was written in the sixth century BC by Daniel.
- Critics find Daniel's book unbelievable because of its prophecy, yet Jesus gave it His endorsement in Matthew 24:15.
- The historical portion teaches God's people how to live in a hostile environment.
- The prophetic portion teaches on "the times of the Gentiles" (see Luke 21:24).

- Daniel uses two writing styles:
  - prophetic
  - historical
- The book was written originally in two languages:
  - Hebrew
  - Aramaic

THE HISTORICAL SECTION—DANIEL 1–6

King Nebuchadnezzar deported a group of Israelites in about 605 BC. This was approximately twenty years before Jerusalem would be destroyed. Daniel was part of this deportation. These were the qualifications for the deportees:
- They must be part of the royal family.
- They must be smart.
- They must be handsome.
- The must be in good health.
- They must be young.

The king wanted to prove that the Babylonian way of life was the best. A great way to do this was to take some of Israel's elite young men and raise them as Babylonians. Isaiah had predicted this a hundred years earlier in Isaiah 39:5–7. Daniel objected to becoming Babylonian because of the Babylonians' overtly pagan ways. Daniel's name was changed, but his character grew deeper over time. In Hebrew, Daniel's name meant "God is judge." In Aramaic, Daniel's new name, Belteshazzar (Daniel 1:7), meant "May Bel protect his life." Bel was the title for a Babylonian god.

Daniel was committed to an undefiled life, and God honored his passion to serve Him in this pagan land. God gave to Daniel and his three companions, Shadrach, Meshach, and Abednego, knowledge and the ability to interpret dreams and visions. These were prevalent in Babylon in his days. Daniel was given wisdom in every matter. Amazingly, Daniel studied in Babylonian schools, dressed like a Babylonian, and had a Babylonian name, yet never compromised. Daniel lived a life of ups and downs in Babylon. In chapter 6, God saved him from the lions in the lions' den, which is one of the most memorable miracles of the Old Testament.

THE PROPHETIC SECTION—DANIEL 7–12

Daniel's visions have meaning for us today. The attached chart helps clarify the times that are laid out for us in each prophecy. Daniel's contribution to an understanding of the end times is immeasurable.

	Dream Image: Daniel 2:31–45 603 BC	1st Vision: 4 Beasts Daniel 7 553 BC	2nd Vision: Ram and Goat Daniel 8 551 BC	3rd Vision: 70 Weeks Daniel 9:24–27 538 BC	4th Vision: Tribulation Daniel 10–12 536 BC
Babylon 605-538 BC	Head of gold (2:32, 37, 38)	Lion (7:4)			
Medo-Persia 538-331 BC	Breast and arms of silver (2:32, 39)	Bear (7:5)	Ram (8:3, 4, 20)	From the commandment going forth—Ezra 458 BC (9:25)	Four Kings (11:2)
Greece 331-146 BC	Belly, thighs of brass (2:32, 39)	Leopard (7:6)	Goat with one horn (8:5, 21) Four horns (8:8, 22) Little horn (8:9–14)	69 weeks continue (9:25)	Mighty king and kingdom divided (11:3,4); Kings of North and South (11:5–20) Vile king Antiochus Epiphanes (11:21–35)
Rome 146 BC- AD 476	Legs of iron; feet of iron and clay (2:33, 40, 41)	Strong Breast (7:7, 11, 19, 23)		Until Messiah is cut off AD 26 (9:26)	
Last Days Yet to Come	Toes of iron/clay (2:33, 42, 43) Stone cut without hands (2:34, 35, 44, 45)	Ten Horns (7:7, 20 ,24); Little Horns (7:8, 20, 21, 24, 26); Reign of Christ (7:13, 14, 18, 22 ,27)	Roman "Beast" prefigured by little horn (8:23–25)	70th week of Tribulation (9:27)	Roman "Beast": Antichrist (11:36–45) Tribulation and its chronology (12:1–13)

Hosea
The Book of Unfaithful Love

OUTLINE
1. Hosea's Experience (1–3)
2. The Message for Israel (4–14)

INTRODUCTION

Hosea begins a new section of Scripture called the Minor Prophets. They are called minor because of their size. Their messages, even though short and concise, are still powerful. The Minor Prophets denounce moral and political corruption fiercely. Hosea prophesied to the northern kingdom of Israel and was a contemporary of Jonah, Amos, and Micah. Hosea lived a sad life to illustrate to the people their unfaithful love for Yahweh.

FAST FACTS

- Hosea wrote his prophetic book around 715 BC.
- The name Hosea means "salvation."
- It is the same as Joshua or Jesus in its roots and meaning.
- Hosea was probably a farmer.
- He was well educated and possessed knowledge of history.
- The message is clear: "God's love for us does not stop even when we fall into sin." Hosea not only preached this message; he lived it.
- The prophet had a tragic marriage that was marred by immorality. This broken marriage covenant is a true picture of Israel and God.

HOSEA'S EXPERIENCE—HOSEA 1–3

God gave a very strange command to the prophet Hosea—to marry a prostitute. This, of course, was forbidden in Israel because of the Law of Moses' strict standards against immoral behavior. Yet God, who created the law, gave the command to Hosea. The prophet obeyed, and he and his wife, Gomer, had children that were named for the coming judgment. Gomer did not repent but, remained a harlot, which is an image of Israel's unfaithfulness. This is a vivid picture of Israel's spiritual adultery.

THE MESSAGE FOR ISRAEL—HOSEA 4-14

The message to the people is clear. There are four points to it:
1. The foolishness of the people (ch 4)
2. The failure of the priests (ch 5)
3. The futility of their shallow repentance (ch 6)
4. The failure of the leaders (ch 7)

God would judge them, yet He would in the future restore them because of His great love. God loves Israel even in the midst of their moral mess. Hosea used the Hebrew term *hesed* for love. It means "loyal love." Just as Hosea truly loved his wayward wife, Yahweh faithfully loves His people, despite their gross sin of idolatry.

Joel
The Book of the Day of the Lord

OUTLINE
1. The Coming Tragedy (1–2:11)
2. The Plea for Repentance (2:12–17)
3. The Promise of Restoration (2:18- 3)

INTRODUCTION

Joel is a small book with a hard-hitting message. With vivid pictures, Joel wrote a masterpiece. The background of the book is a terrible locust invasion, which occurred in the land of Judah. Joel used this plague to describe the future invasion of "the Day of the Lord."

FAST FACTS

- Joel wrote the book around 835 BC.
- Joel means "Jehovah is my God."
- He was a contemporary of Elijah and Elisha.
- The book is noted for four things:
    1. Its graphic description of the locust invasion (1:6–10, 2:1–10)
    2. Its insight into the Day of the Lord (2:28–3:31)
    3. Its description of the outpouring of God's Spirit (2:28–29)
    4. Its prophecies. (1:15; 3:14)

THE COMING TRAGEDY—JOEL 1–2:11

The locust invasion is seen in four stages. Perhaps there were four different types of locusts that ate their way through Judah. Joel gave the people ten things that they should do beginning in verse 13: repent, weep, wail, and so on.

THE PLEA FOR REPENTANCE—JOEL 2:12-17
God passionately called His covenant people back to Him. Their return could only be done God's way: "With all your heart." If the people would rally together under the banner of repentance, God would take pity on His land.

THE PROMISE OF RESTORATION—JOEL 2:18-3
The people would one day be restored. The land would be revived. They would prosper again. The Spirit's outpouring would come, as Peter spoke about in Acts 2:16. This has partially been fulfilled but will be fulfilled in full in the coming messianic kingdom after the Day of the Lord.

Amos
The Book of Woes

OUTLINE
1. Prophecies Concerning the Nations (1–2)
2. Sermons Denouncing Israel (3–6)
3. Visions of Restoration (7–9)

INTRODUCTION

Amos prophesied sometime during the years that Jeroboam II was ruling in Israel and Uzziah was ruling in Judah. He was a contemporary of Hosea in the north and Isaiah in the south.

Israel was at the peak of her prosperity from 765 to 740 BC. The rich had amassed their wealth at the expense of the poor. Judges sold justice to the highest bidder. Merchants were notorious for dishonesty. Immorality and idolatry were practiced openly and shamelessly. The relevance of Amos to our current affluent society is obvious.

FAST FACTS

- The author is Amos. He wrote the book around 755 BC.
- Amos means "burden."
- Amos was uneducated and a shepherd by trade.
- From Tekoa, which was just southeast of Bethlehem, Amos lived in the southern nation of Judah. Yet, God called him to preach to the northern tribes of Israel. This was no doubt a tough ministry because of the ill feelings between the two nations.
- Amos also was a grower of sycamore figs (7:14) and could be described as a common man. So, the ministry of Amos is that of a simple, faithful man going up against the socially and financially elite of the prosperous Northern Kingdom, which saw little need for Yahweh worship.
- For a period of about a year, Amos gave God's message to the Northern Kingdom. His ministry was two years before a notable earthquake.

Archaeological excavations at Hazor and Samaria have uncovered evidence of a violent earthquake in Israel in 760 BC.

PROPHECIES CONCERNING THE NATIONS—AMOS 1-2

Amos reveals that the wrath of the Lord "roars from Zion" (1:2). He was going to repay the neighboring nations of Israel. He would "send fire" to each of them (v. 4):
- to Syria for cruelty (1:3-5)
- to Philistia for slavery (1:6-8)
- to Phoenicia for treaty breaking (1:9-10)
- to Edom for revenge (1:11-12)
- to Ammon for violence (1:13-15)
- to Moab for evil (2:1-3)

God would not turn away or cancel the punishment. The people were going to be judged:
- Judah for despising the law (2:4-5)
- Israel for immorality and blasphemy (2:6-16)

SERMONS DENOUNCING ISRAEL—AMOS 3-6

Amos next delivered three sermons for Israel that uncovered their sinful lifestyle.

VISIONS OF RESTORATION—AMOS 7-9

Amos then was given five visions that pictured the judgment. They are:
1. Vision of grasshoppers (7:1-3)
2. Vision of fire (7:4-6)
3. Vision of the plumb line (7:7-9)
4. Vision of the summer fruit (8)
5. Vision of the Lord and the altar (9:1-10)

The book concludes with God's marvelous promise of restoration (9:11-15). God uses "I wills" to underscore the security of His promises.

Obadiah
The Book of Warning

OUTLINE
1. Edom's Doom (1:1–16)
2. Israel's Deliverance (1:17–21)

INTRODUCTION
Obadiah is the shortest book of the Old Testament and is not quoted in the New Testament. It appears to be the forgotten book of the Old Testament. It deals with Edom and their coming judgment for gloating over Israel's misfortunes.

FAST FACTS
- Little is known about the author, and the date of writing is also hard to establish. Our best estimate is that Obadiah wrote the book in 841 BC.
- Obadiah means "servant of Jehovah," and this name is shared with twelve other people in the Old Testament.
- The Edomites were descendants of Esau, and they were a continual thorn in Israel's side.

EDOM'S DOOM—OBADIAH 1–1:16
Despite their hidden location, God would judge Edom, and they would not escape. In verse 3, Obadiah talks of the Edomites hiding in the "clefts of the rocks." The area of Edom is in modern-day southern Jordan. Even though Petra is one of the best places to hide in the Middle East, the Edomites were going to be found and dealt with.

ISRAEL'S DELIVERANCE—OBADIAH 1:17–21
Israel was in rubble but would have a great future. God rebuked the pride of the Edomites, and the Romans would later obliterate them. Yet for Israel,

deliverance would be seen on Mount Zion. The book of Obadiah is about retribution for cursing Israel. God promised in Genesis 12 to curse anyone who cursed Israel, His covenant people.

Jonah

The Book of God's Forgiveness

OUTLINE
1. Jonah's First Commission (1–2)
2. Jonah's Second Commission (3–4)

INTRODUCTION

This book is unlike any of the other Minor Prophets. Its style and content are that of a historical narrative. The book centers around God's dealings with the prophet rather than on the message itself. Perhaps more than any other book in the Bible, Jonah has been assailed by critics. The current theory is to laugh the book out of the Bible. The critical theologian finds three things absolutely unpalatable in the historical narrative:
1. The great fish
2. The sudden repentance of Nineveh
3. The remarkable growth of the gourd

Critical theories on the book are too numerous to list, yet all of them are shattered by Matthew 12:39–40, which says, *"He answered, 'A wicked and adulterous generation asks for a sign! But none will be given it except the sign of the prophet Jonah. For as Jonah was three days and three nights in the belly of a huge fish, so the Son of Man will be three days and three nights in the heart of the earth.'"* Jesus endorsed the book of Jonah, so that's all the proof anyone needs as to its validity.

FAST FACTS

- The author, Jonah, was a real prophet. *"He was the one who restored the boundaries of Israel from Lebo Hamath to the Dead Sea, in accordance with the word of the LORD, the God of Israel, spoken through his servant Jonah son of Amittai, the prophet from Gath Hepher"* (2 Kings 14:25).
- The title means "Dove." It was written around 760 BC.

- There are similarities to Paul, the New Testament leader: both were missionaries; both had a wild ship ride, and both saved sailors' lives.
- Jonah is called to an area roughly five hundred miles east of Palestine, yet he ventures to go two *thousand* miles west.
- Jonah is one of the four Old Testament prophets referred to by Jesus. The other three were Elijah, Elisha, and Isaiah.
- Some say Jonah couldn't have written the book because he is referred to in the third person! This is not a good argument though, since Moses did this in the Pentateuch to refer to his own actions. Isaiah and Daniel also did this.

JONAH'S FIRST COMMISSION—JONAH 1-2

Jonah is given a divine command by God. Jonah goes the opposite way to escape his calling by God to the Assyrians. The Assyrians, according to history, were the cruelest of empires. Their torture and murder knew no bounds. Entire villages committed suicide when they heard that the Assyrian Ninevites were on their way.

God's mighty hand over creation is seen in His control over the storm and over the great fish. Jonah saw seven miracles before turning to total obedience.

JONAH'S SECOND COMMISSION—JONAH 3-4

Jehovah is the God of the second chance. After causing Jonah to spend three days in the belly of the great fish, God now had his attention. Amazingly, Jonah preached an eight-word sermon, and the people repented. God's Word is powerful: the people repented wholeheartedly. The people did not delay, and their repentance was genuine.

The last chapter is the real message of the book. Jonah has a conversation with Jehovah. Jonah is displeased that the Ninevites repented. God shows him that He is the God of the Gentiles too.

Micah

The Book of Sin, Suffering, and Salvation

OUTLINE
1. Message to the Nations (1–2)
2. Message to the Rulers (3–5)
3. Message to the People (6–7)

INTRODUCTION

Micah was a contemporary of Isaiah. Like Isaiah, this prophecy is a beautiful and moving example of Hebrew literature. Isaiah was the court poet, while Micah was a rustic from an obscure village.

Isaiah	Micah
Statesman	Evangelist and social reformer
Voice to Kings	Voice to common people
Addressed political questions	Addressed social questions

Micah vigorously condemned Israel and Judah because of their great wickedness and then announced their punishment; he then prophesied a subsequent restoration into God's favor. Somewhat unique is Micah's condemnation of many social sins rather than the sin of idolatry.

FAST FACTS

- Micah wrote the book around 700 BC.
- Micah was from Moresheth, twenty-five miles southwest of Jerusalem.
- Micah has a dominant theme: "The chosen people's sin will not prevent the accomplishment of God's purpose through them."
- God's standard of measurement in the book of Micah is Israel's failure to live up to the Mosaic covenant.

- Deuteronomy detailed the covenantal scriptures for blessing or cursing from Deuteronomy 28.
- Micah announced that God was just in disciplining them.
- Micah spoke of a group within the nation who continued to seek to live for God, called "the remnant."
- Much of the book was written in poetry and reads much like portions of Psalms, with a style called *parallelism*.
- Two thoughts within one sentence are either compared or contrasted to illustrate a point.
- Micah also contains six amazing predictions:
  1. The destruction of Samaria
  2. The destruction of Jerusalem
  3. Babylonian captivity
  4. Return from captivity
  5. The birth and birthplace of the Messiah
  6. The coming kingdom.

MESSAGE TO THE NATIONS – MICAH 1–2

Micah delivers a message to the nations that were due a judgment of God because of their idolatry. The people of Israel were subject to false prophets, who spoke their own words.

MESSAGE TO THE RULERS—MICAH 3–5

The princes, prophets, and priests were all corrupt. The princes had no compassion. The prophets preached falsely. The priests could be bought for money. The leadership of Israel was evil to the core.

MESSAGE TO THE PEOPLE—MICAH 6–7

God asked the people how He has been a burden to them. The crux of the book is found in Micah 6:8, where God described real spirituality: "He has showed you, O mortal, what is good. And what does the Lord require of you? To act justly and to love mercy and to walk humbly with your God."

The spiritual person will have true inner change of the heart.

Nahum
The Book of God's Judgment

 **OUTLINE**
1. The Lord against Nineveh (1)
2. Nineveh's Judgment (2–3)

INTRODUCTION

Two of God's prophets dealt with Nineveh, the great capital of the Assyrian Empire. Jonah prophesied about 785 BC. The prophets were about 135 years apart. In the intervening 135 years, the ten northern tribes had been carried into captivity; and God patiently gave the Ninevites opportunity to repent. Now the day of grace had ended, and the moment of doom had arrived. Assyria had served God's purpose and now was going to be destroyed. The accuracy of Nahum's predictions were verified forty years later.

Nahum wrote in classic Hebrew poetry style, with vivid descriptions. His tone is intense, to say the least.

FAST FACTS
- Nahum wrote the book between 663 and 612 BC.
- Nahum means "comforter," and the theme is "God's wrath is slow but devastating."
- Nahum was from Elkosh, which was possibly close to Capernaum in Galilee.

BACKGROUND:
1. When Nahum uttered this prophecy, Assyria was at its height.
2. Shalmaneser II and Sargon laid waste to the Northern Kingdom and taxed the Southern Kingdom excessively.
3. Sennacherib would have taken Jerusalem, yet Hezekiah prayed and God answered! The Angel of the Lord killed more than 185,000 Assyrians.

4. Nineveh was the queen city of the earth. It was the center for commerce, wealth, and prestige.

THE CITY:
Nineveh's importance was centered around the cult of Ishtar. Immoral practices were a part of this pagan worship.

Six World Powers of Bible Times
1. Egypt
2. Assyria
3. Babylon
4. Medo-Persia
5. Greece
6. Rome

- The destruction of Nineveh was so complete that Alexander the Great fought the battle of Arbela (or, Gaugamela) nearby in 331 BC and did not know a city had even been there.
- Napoleon camped on it, unaware of the city's ruins beneath him.

FACTS ABOUT NINEVEH
- Archaeological discoveries have revealed brick walls fifty feet thick, one hundred feet high.
- Assyria was probably the most feared nation of all time. Historical records reveal entire cities committing suicide before the Assyrians arrived. Some of Assyria's victims were skinned alive like animals.
- Nineveh was famous for witchcraft and immorality. Public nudity was normal.
- Nahum uttered this prophecy while Assyria was at its zenith! Do you think Nahum's prophecies were easy to believe at the time?

THE LORD AGAINST NINEVEH—NAHUM 1
Some very pleasant words concerning the Lord's character are revealed in chapter 1:
Verse 3—"The LORD is slow to anger and great in power."
Verse 7—"The LORD is good, a refuge in times of trouble. He cares for those who trust in him."

Yet God would conclusively would wipe out Nineveh, and it would be a cause of celebration in Israel: "*Celebrate your festivals, Judah, and fulfill your vows. No more will the wicked invade you; they will be completely destroyed*" (v. 15).

NINEVEH'S JUDGMENT—NAHUM 2-3

Nineveh would be a nation that came up against the Holy One of Israel and lost. Because of their immoral worship, which involved sexual depravity, God was going to reveal their nakedness to the world. In 612 BC, the combined armies of the Babylonians and the Medes annihilated Nineveh exactly as God had promised.

Habakkuk

The Book of Faith

OUTLINE
1. Faith Tested (1)
2. Faith Taught (2)
3. Faith Triumphant (3)

INTRODUCTION

This book is one of complaint rather than a prediction or a condemnation of sin. Unlike the other prophets, Habakkuk did not address either his own countrymen or a foreign people. He directed his speech to God alone. His main burden was the solving of a very perplexing problem: Why was God silent when wickedness prevailed on every hand? Men seemed to be defying God and getting away with it.

FAST FACTS
- Habakkuk wrote the book about 606 BC.
- Habakkuk has often been referred to as "the free-thinker among the prophets" because he actually questioned the government of God.[23]
- He could not reconcile a good and righteous God with the facts of life as he saw them.
- He was the philosopher of prophets.
- The title means "embracing or caressing"; God embraced His people as one embracing a child.
- We know nothing about the author except his name. Yet, he shows intimate knowledge of the priesthood. He may even have been a priest.
- The theme of the book is "the just shall live by faith" (see Habakkuk 2:4 in the King James Version). We operate the same way today. Three New Testament writings use this theme (note that the NIV substitutes "righteous" for "just"):

1. Romans 1:17
2. Galatians 3:11
3. Hebrews 10:38

FAITH TESTED—HABAKKUK 1

Habakkuk questioned the Lord boldly about injustice. Why did God allow sin to continue? Why did the righteous suffer, and the wicked didn't? The prophet was dissatisfied with God's answers as He was prepared to use the Babylonians to straighten out wayward Israel.

FAITH TAUGHT—HABAKKUK 2

Habakkuk positioned himself on the rampart walls of Jerusalem to wait for God's answer. God always answers the honest in heart, and He did with Habakkuk also. God had a plan for their present misery. God commanded silence before Him.

FAITH TRIUMPHANT—HABAKKUK 3

Habakkuk pleaded with God to actively perform the miraculous in his day. God gave him a vision of who He was. Habakkuk realized that he could trust God after all.

Zephaniah
The Book of Divine Wrath

OUTLINE
1. God's Wrath on Judah (1–2:3)
2. God's Wrath on the Nations (2:4–3:8)
3. God's Restoration of All (3:9–20)

INTRODUCTION
Approximately one hundred years had passed since the fall of the Northern Kingdom; and conditions in Judah were pretty much like the conditions that had prevailed in Israel just before their captivity.

Egypt, Assyria, and Babylon were striving for supremacy. Some of Judah's leaders felt that there should have been an alliance with one of these powers, while others insisted upon a policy of strict isolationism.

As Zephaniah looked around at the religious life of the people, he found foreign priests and altars to Baal springing up all over the land. Even the short revival under Josiah had not halted the impending judgment. The day of God's wrath was imminent, as in Obadiah and Joel.

FAST FACTS
- The author, Zephaniah, was of royal descent. He wrote the book about 640–621 BC.
- The title means "Jehovah hides."
- King Josiah reigned at that time.
- Zephaniah was contemporary with Jeremiah and Nahum.
- The theme is "God's love expressed by wrath," a means of purifying His people for their future good.

GOD'S WRATH ON JUDAH—ZEPHANIAH 1–2:3
The great day of the Lord was on its way. God judges His own people first and then unbelievers next. The great day of the Lord in verses 14–18 appears to go beyond the devastation of the day and points to a future catastrophic event. Verse 18 speaks of the whole world being consumed.

GOD'S WRATH ON THE NATIONS—ZEPHANIAH 2:4–3:8
Yahweh lists the nations doomed to the coming judgment.

GOD'S RESTORATION OF ALL—ZEPHANIAH 3:9–20
The future restoration of God's people and the city of Jerusalem is foretold. God would bring His people back with shouts of joy to Zion.

Old Testament

Haggai
The Book of Duty

OUTLINE
1. Message of Rebuke (1)
2. Message of Encouragement and Blessing (2:1–19)
3. Message of Hope (2:20–23)

INTRODUCTION
We come now to a new period of Old Testament history—the time after the Jews returned from their captivity. Therefore Haggai, Zechariah, and Malachi are referred to as post-exilic prophets. The history of this period is given in the books of Ezra and Nehemiah.

Haggai is mentioned in Ezra 5:1 and 6:14 along with Zechariah as the prophet who encouraged the remnant and who returned after the Babylonian captivity, to rebuild the temple while in the midst of difficulties. As his book reveals, he was evidently a very practical man.

FAST FACTS
- The author, Haggai, was probably born in Babylon and returned with Zerubbabel. He was a contemporary with Zechariah and maybe Malachi. He was a layman used by God. He wrote his book in 520 BC to the people of Jerusalem.
- The title means "my feast."
- The theme is "Put God first in all things!" The spiritual Jews returned, so they were considered good Jews. They returned to rebuild the temple, but they got sidetracked.

THE MESSAGE OF REBUKE—HAGGAI 1
Haggai chastised the people for living in expensive paneled houses while God's house lay in ruins. God said, "I am with you" in the rebuilding of the temple.

THE MESSAGE OF ENCOURAGEMENT AND BLESSING—HAGGAI 2:1-19

God promised that the glory of the new temple would be greater than the glory of the former temple. This seemed improbable at the time, since the temple was significantly smaller than the first one. This would come true, of course, as King Herod enlarged the temple in Jesus' day to colossal proportions. God covenanted to bless the people from this day on.

THE MESSAGE OF HOPE—HAGGAI 2:20-23

God gave Governor Zerubbabel His authority to complete the temple. God's authority was going to smash all foreign kingdoms one day.

Zechariah
The Book of Vision and Victory

> OUTLINE
> 1. The Proclamations (1–6)
> 2. The Practicals (7–8)
> 3. The Predictions (9–14)

INTRODUCTION

The purpose of Zechariah's ministry was similar to that of Haggai's—namely, to encourage the people to rebuild the temple. However, their methods were quite different. Haggai was a practical man who exhorted the people to work. Zechariah was a visionary man who furnished the incentive to work through a revelation of Israel's glorious future.

Zechariah unfolded the events connected with the first and second advents of the Messiah. It is the most messianic book and most apocalyptic of all the writings of the Old Testament.

His visions remind us of Daniel and Revelation.

FAST FACTS

- The author, Zechariah, was a prophet and descendant of the priestly line of Aaron. His ministry lasted only three years. He wrote the book between 520 and 518 BC.
- The title Zechariah means "God remembers."
- The theme is "Repent and serve God with your whole heart–a glorious future is ahead!"

THE PROCLAMATIONS—ZECHARIAH 1-6
Zechariah's Eight Night Visions

Vision	Reference	Meaning
The Red Horse Rider Among the Myrtles	1:7-17	God's anger against the nations and blessing on restored Israel.
The Four Horns and the Four Craftsmen	1:18-21	God's judgment on the nations that had afflicted Israel.
The Surveyor with a Measuring Line	2	God's future blessing on a restored Israel.
The Cleansing and Crowning of Joshua, the High Priest	3	Israel's future cleansing from sin and reinstatement as a priestly nation.
The Gold Lampstand and the Two Olive Trees	4	Israel as the light to the nations under Messiah, the King-Priest.
The Flying Scroll	5:1-4	The severity and totality of divine judgment on individual Israelites.
The Woman in the Measuring Basket	5:5-11	The removal of Israel's sin of rebellion against God.
The Four Chariots	6:1-8	Divine judgment on Gentile nations

THE PRACTICALS—ZECHARIAH 7-8

The people asked the Lord if they were to continue fasting, as they had done for seventy years. The carnal man seeks ritual because it makes him feel holy. God gave three answers to their question:

1. When the heart is right, ritual is right (7:4-7).
2. When the heart is wrong, ritual is wrong (7:8-14).
3. God's purpose is unchanged by ritual (8).

Holiness is developed internally, not externally.

THE PREDICTIONS—ZECHARIAH 9-14

This section contains one of the Old Testament's major passages on the first and second comings of the Messiah. This develops fully God's plan for Israel, which will culminate with the return of Jesus the Messiah. He will deliver Israel from "all the nations" of the world (14:2), which will gather together to destroy Israel, and Jerusalem in particular. This glorious day will bring an end to the tribulation and an end to Israel's enemies.

Malachi
The Book of Rebuke and Hope

OUTLINE
1. God's Love Acclaimed (1:1-5)
2. God's Condemnation Affirmed (1:6-3:18)
3. God's Comfort Assured (4)

INTRODUCTION

Nehemiah wrote the last history of the Old Testament, so Malachi gives us the last prophecy. Once the voice of Malachi died out, there was silence for four hundred years. That silence was broken by John the Baptist, and his message was "I am the voice of one calling in the wilderness. Make straight the way for the Lord" (John 1:23; cf. Matthew 3:3).

Malachi's emphasis is upon the Day of the Lord with its twofold message of judgment and deliverance. His message deals with certain evils practiced by the Jews.

The people were now completely irreverent, and their sarcasm is a picture of their prideful heart even in the face of judgment.

FAST FACTS
- The author, Malachi, may have been a priest and had a knowledge of the priesthood.
- Malachi wrote the book in 430 BC to the Jews in Jerusalem.
- The title means "my messenger" or "my angel."
- The theme is God's unfailing love, seen in two ways:
  1. Blessing
  2. Rebuke

GOD'S LOVE ACCLAIMED—MALACHI 1:1-5

God gave a final oracle through Malachi to close the Old Testament. An oracle means "a burden." The message was a heavy one. God declared that He had loved Israel, yet they had not loved Him in return.

GOD'S CONDEMNATION AFFIRMED—MALACHI 1:6-3:18

The sacrifices brought to holy God were second best and, therefore, unacceptable to Him. The animals they offered were unclean and defiled because they were crippled and diseased. The fire on the altar was useless. The only time in Scripture God calls His people to "test" Him on something is in Malachi 3:10. The subject is tithing, and God promises to bless the faithful tither.

GOD'S COMFORT ASSURED—MALACHI 4

The Old Testament ends with the promise of a coming prophet in the spirit of Elijah. God, after four hundred years of silence, would send John the Baptist and shatter the quiet, as he would be the forerunner of the Messiah. The Old Testament ends with a curse in verse 5, and Jesus the Messiah would shatter that curse upon His arrival four centuries years later.

The Period Between the Testaments

Year	Event
400 B.C.	Malachi
300-30 B.C	Apocryphal books written
323 B.C.	Alexander the Great dies
280-200	Septuagint written
200 B.C.	Great Wall of China built
167 B.C.	Antiochus Epiphanes defiles the temple in Jerusalem by offering swine flesh on Hebrew altar
165 B.C.	The temple cleansed and reopened by Judas Maccabees
63 B.C.	Pompey takes Jerusalem
44 B.C.	Julius Caesar assassinated
37 B.C.	Herod the Great begins to govern Palestine
37 B.C.	Herod the Great rebuilds Jerusalem
5 B.C.	Jesus Born
4 B.C.	Herod the Great dies

NEW TESTAMENT

Matthew
The Gospel of the Messiah

OUTLINE
1. The Presentation of the King (1–4:11)
2. The Proclamation of the King (4:12–7:29)
3. The Power of the King (8–11:1)
4. The Opposition of the King (11:2–27:66)
5. The Proof of the King (28)

INTRODUCTION
The book of Matthew is the first book of the New Testament and is the first book of the four Gospels. Gospel means "good news."

Why Four Gospels?
All New Testament books had to be written by an apostle or backed by an apostle. Numerous gospel accounts were written—only four, however, were inspired by God, and they became obvious to the early church. Each Gospel targeted a specific group; they are as follows:
- Matthew (to the Jews)
- Mark (to the Romans)
- Luke (to other Gentiles)
- John (to Christians)

FAST FACTS
- The author, Matthew, was a Palestinian Jew, as is evident from his thorough knowledge of Palestinian geography. He was an educated man and was a tax collector, probably under Herod Antipas. It was written between 50 AD-70 AD.
- Matthew appears as a wealthy man who was humbled by Jesus; he repented and became one of the Twelve. He referred to himself as a "tax collec-

tor" (9:9; the King James Version uses the word "publican"). Taxes were done according to a five-year census. "Tax farming" was an easy way for Rome to collect its funds and stimulate business also. An auction was held to determine who would collect the assigned taxes for Rome. Once this was determined, the collector used whatever means he wanted to collect, and he set the taxes high enough to ensure a healthy profit for himself. Tax collectors were despised (9:10–11). Matthew was considered low-class in people's eyes. He had sold out to Rome and cheated his own people!
- Matthew preached the gospel for about fourteen years after Jesus rose from the dead. His mission field was to the Syrians, Medes, and Persians. His purpose was to show unbelieving Jews that Jesus is the Messiah and to encourage Jewish believers.

THE PRESENTATION OF THE KING—MATTHEW 1–4:11

Jesus is the main person of this Gospel, and the first verse of the book connects Him with the two great covenants of Israel's history.
- Abrahamic covenant—Genesis 12:1–3: "All peoples on earth will be blessed through you" (v. 3).
- Davidic covenant—2 Samuel 7:12–13: "I will establish the throne of his kingdom forever" (v. 13).

The first question for any Jew would have been "Is He of the right line?" The answer, of course, was yes. Matthew gave the lineage of Jesus through Joseph. Jesus had a claim to the throne of David. Matthew lists fourteen generations, three times. Each generation is laid out in chapter 1. They extend:
- from Abraham to David
- from David to the exile
- from the exile to Christ

Joseph's betrothed, Mary, was pregnant out of wedlock—and not by him. Though he did not know it yet, the child conceived in her was "from the Holy Spirit." In Matthew 1, Joseph had two choices with Mary:
- He could divorce her privately.
- He could have her stoned.

As an honorable man, Joseph married Mary, (due to an angelic visitation, 1:20) and only understood the gravity of the miracle of her conception later. The story of their baby's birth is found in chapter 2, where Magi called him the "king of the Jews" (v. 2).

Herod the king fancied himself the king of the Jews and reacted strongly to the news that "another" king of the Jews was now here. His slaughter of all the male babies two years old and younger was typical of his rule.

In chapter 3, an adult Jesus was baptized; and in chapter 4, he conclusively defeated Satan using the Word of God three times.

THE PROCLAMATIONS OF THE KING—MATTHEW 4:12–7:29

Jesus used the phrase "Truly I tell you" thirty-one times in Matthew's Gospel, proving He had come in authority from heaven to teach God's ways. The people were religious yet lost in the formalities of their religion. Jesus burst through their false belief system with the greatest sermon ever recorded. The Sermon on the Mount brought the kingdom of God to the common Israelite. Rejecting the pride and legalism of the religious elite of the day, Jesus taught the people the way to God.

THE POWER OF THE KING—MATTHEW 8–11:1

Jesus preached with power and authority, but would He back it up? Conclusively, Jesus healed the diseased, cast out the demons, raised the dead, and proved He was God in the flesh in this section. Jesus shocked the Pharisees by forgiving sin, which could only be done by God Himself.

THE OPPOSITION OF THE KING—MATTHEW 11:2–27:66

Jesus reacted to the mounting opposition knowing that the hardened hearts of the religious would finally kill Him. Despite the hardened hearts of the Pharisees, scribes, and priests, they continued to ask for Jesus to perform miracles. Jesus denied their request and told them in 12:39–40 that there would be one more miracle—the resurrection.

The death of Jesus was cruel, inhumane, and illegal according to Roman law. The religious leaders whipped the angry mob into a frenzy, and they killed Jesus in one of the most torturous ways. The Romans who occupied Israel during Jesus' days crucified thousands during their rule. The victim would eventually die by suffocation. Jesus died on Passover Day, AD 30, as the final Lamb of God, sacrificed for our sin. His blood is what can cleanse everyone from their sins.

The religious leaders figured they were done with Jesus for good. Three days later, they found out they were wrong.

THE PROOF OF THE KING—MATTHEW 28:1-20

Matthew 28 is Jesus' victory cry over the grave. His resurrection is the anchor of our faith. Jesus defeated the grave. Jesus bore our sins on the cross and paid the sacrifice necessary to secure forgiveness. God Himself accepted Jesus' sacrifice for our sins. Everyone who repents of their sins, believes Jesus is the Messiah, and receives Him by faith can be born again and spend their eternity in heaven with Christ. Matthew, the writer of this book, experienced this. He was a despised tax collector known for cheating fellow Jews. He was the lowest of the low in Israel. Yet, in Matthew 9:9, God called Matthew with two simple words, "Follow me!" Matthew left his evil ways and followed Jesus, his Master for life. Matthew never forgot his background. As he listed the disciples in his Gospel, he referred to himself as "Matthew the tax collector" (10:3). Matthew is proof that Jesus is the Messiah and can radically transform even the worst of sinners.

Mark
The Gospel of the Servant

OUTLINE
1. The Servant Revealed (1–3:5)
2. The Servant Rejected (3:6–15:47)
3. The Servant Resurrected (16)

INTRODUCTION

The purpose of the Gospel of Mark appears to focus on Jesus Christ's life of servanthood here on earth. Matthew's aim was to present the overwhelming testimony of Jesus Christ as the Messiah coming forth from and for Israel. Mark's record is far less Jewish in thought. It excludes:
- the Sermon on the Mount
- Christ's genealogy
- condemnation of Jewish traditionalists

Mark has been called the Gospel of Action. Twelve of the sixteen chapters begin with *Kai*, the Greek word for "and." The central theme verse is Mark 10:45: *"For even the Son of Man did not come to be served, but to serve and to give his life as a ransom for many."* This holds forth to the reader the very thought of the writer as to the significance and purpose of his biography of Jesus Christ—the servant.

Some of the unique characteristics of Mark's Gospel are these:
- historical present—Matthew wrote in the present tense for past action.
- the emphasis on miracles
- vivid details

The two miracles found only in Mark are
- healing of the deaf mute of Decapolis (Mark 7)
- healing of the blind man at Bethsaida (Mark 8)

Mark wrote from Rome, where the apostle Peter died, and he targeted the Roman audience. Since Mark wrote to this non-Jewish group, it explained the Gospel's lack of Jewish culture. Here are some examples:
- The Old Testament is quoted very little.
- Mark explains Jewish customs.
- There is no mention of the Mosaic law.
- Mark explains where the Mount of Olives was.
- He emphasized the power of the will.

FAST FACTS
- John Mark wrote his Gospel between AD 50 and 60.
- John Mark had a tough experience on Paul's first missionary journey. Perhaps due to his young age, the trials he faced proved to be overwhelming. Later on, after traveling with Barnabas, his cousin, John Mark and Paul came to an agreement; and the fellowship was restored.
- In 2 Timothy 4:11, Paul wrote, "Get Mark and bring him with you, because he is helpful to me in my ministry." Paul was asking Timothy to bring John Mark for one last visit before the great apostle went home to be with the Lord.
- John Mark established a personal relationship with Peter in Rome. At the end of Peter's life, he called Mark "my son" in 1 Peter 5:13. Mark's Gospel is an eyewitness account, which probably came through long conversations with Peter, who was present at all the events listed.
- The young man who escaped from the Garden of Gethsemane minus his clothes was probably young John Mark.

THE SERVANT REVEALED—MARK 1–3:5
The Gospel begins with John the Baptist crying out in the wilderness. He announced the coming of the Messiah and called the people to repentance in preparation for His arrival. In chapter 1, the most action-packed day of Jesus' ministry is recorded. In the Gospels, fifty-two days of Jesus' life are recorded. This one is by far the longest. Jesus' power over disease, demons, and deformity was quickly established. The people were astonished at his authority.

THE SERVANT REJECTED—MARK 3:6-15:47

This section of the book highlights Jesus' miracles of power. His authority over the storm while on the Sea of Galilee proved He is ruler over nature itself. Jesus also encountered a demonized man that had numerous evil spirits attached to him. He delivered the man easily from the demons. Jesus also fed five thousand people with five loaves of bread and two fish. He proved that He was the Creator by multiplying the modest amount of food to enormous proportions. During this time of ministry, the religious leaders of Israel decide to kill Jesus.

Jesus' last weeks of His earthly life were spent in Jerusalem, teaching, and in late-night prayer vigils. After the Last Supper, with his disciples, and His prayer session in the Garden of Gethsemane, Jesus was arrested, beaten, and condemned to death. Jesus was next nailed to a Roman cross for our sins. On the cross, He confirmed His own words in Mark 10:45: "For even the Son of Man did not come to be served, but to serve and to give his life as a ransom for many."

THE RESURRECTION OF THE SERVANT—MARK 16

The Gospel of Action concludes with the greatest miracle of all time—the glorious resurrection. Mark records Jesus' ascension into heaven and the disciples' spreading of the gospel, accompanied by great signs and wonders.

NEW TESTAMENT

Luke
The Gospel of the Gentiles

OUTLINE
1. Jesus' Birth and Preparation (1–4:13)
2. Jesus' Ministry (4:14–21:38)
3. Jesus' Sacrifice and Resurrection (22–24:53)

INTRODUCTION

Luke is the only Gentile author of scripture. He was a doctor and a close friend of the apostle Paul. Under the guidance of the Holy Spirit, Luke combined the testimony of eyewitnesses and servants of Christ and compiled his gospel. Luke was not an eyewitness of the life of Christ, like Matthew and John. In 1:3, Luke tells us that he wrote a complete orderly account of what he had learned about Jesus. He addressed the book to Theophilus, likely an important person of high rank. His name means "friend of God."

FAST FACTS

- Luke wrote this Gospel and also the book of the Acts of the Apostles.
- The book of Luke was written in AD 60.
- Luke is the most technical work of the four Gospels.
- Luke became a missionary and traveled with Paul as an evangelist.
- Paul in 2 Timothy 4:11 wrote that Luke was his only companion at the end of his life.
- Luke is unique in that he gives the most complete account of Jesus' birth (and also John the Baptist's birth). It is believed that his detailed treatment of the event was given to him by Mary, the mother of Jesus.

JESUS' BIRTH AND PREPARATION—LUKE 1–4:13

The incarnation of Jesus was the event that led to salvation and is available to the whole world. *Incarnation* means "with flesh." In other words, God became flesh, or one of us. Luke gave the priest Zechariah's prophecy concerning his son, John the Baptist, and his message of forgiveness before the Messiah would arrive.

Jesus' birth was accompanied by many angelic visits. When He was born, angels appeared in the sky, praising God. An angel also appeared to shepherds in the fields of Bethlehem. Luke also told of righteous Simeon's dramatic meeting with baby Jesus at the temple. He had spent the greater part of his life waiting for the Savior's arrival. Jesus grew up, and by chapters 3 and 4, He was now a man and was baptized and withstood Satan's temptations.

JESUS' MINISTRY—LUKE 4:14–21:38

Jesus came bursting on the scene in Nazareth as He opened the scroll and read the daily passage in the synagogue under the power of the Holy Spirit. The passage He read was Isaiah 61, a messianic reading that would be fulfilled through Jesus' life. Jesus proclaimed, "Today this scripture is fulfilled in your hearing" (4:21). The people were furious and tried to push him off a steep cliff outside Nazareth. Jesus miraculously walked right through the crowd. His life was not going to be taken until He was ready to give it up for our sins.

Jesus demonstrated His power over demons, diseases, and sin itself. He had unique dialogues with a lawyer, which led to the parable of the good Samaritan. This was an important teaching in that the Jews despised the Samaritans, yet the Samaritan in Jesus' story handled an injured Jew in a godly way. He, rather than the priest or the Levite in Jesus' parable, was the example of how to live.

JESUS' SACRIFICE AND RESURRECTION—LUKE 22–24:53

Luke covered the last week of Jesus' life and gave special attention to His death and burial. Again, Luke points out two Gentiles who had a special ministry with Jesus. Simon the Cyrene carried Jesus' cross when He could no longer lift it. Joseph of Arimathea took Jesus' body and carefully prepared it for burial. He wrapped it in linen cloth and placed it in a tomb in which no one had ever been buried. Chapter 24 records the day of rejoicing as Jesus rose victoriously over sin and death. His resurrection culminated with sightings of the physically risen Savior on the Emmaus road and during a meal with the disciples. Luke followed Jesus all the way to the ascension from the Mount of Olives into heaven.

John
The Gospel of Belief

OUTLINE
1. The Presentation of Jesus (1–16)
2. The Intercession of Jesus (17)
3. The Crucifixion of Jesus (18–19:42)
4. The Resurrection of Jesus (20–21)

INTRODUCTION

John is the disciple "whom Jesus loved" (John 13:23; 21:7; 21:20; cf. 19:26). He was called "son of thunder" along with his brother, James (see Mark 3:17). John was one of the "inner three" that Jesus often spent time with away from the rest of the disciples. The others were Peter and James, and they were eyewitnesses to the transfiguration. He reflected this in 1:14 when he said, "And we beheld his glory" (RSV). John was the only disciple to not face a martyr's death.

John clearly spelled out why he wrote the Gospel at the end of his book. John 20:30–31 says, *"Jesus performed many other signs in the presence of his disciples, which are not recorded in this book. But these are written that you may believe that Jesus is the Messiah, the Son of God, and that by believing you may have life in his name.."* John wrote the Gospel of Belief and included eight miracles that prove Jesus is Lord and Savior.

FAST FACTS

- John wrote the Gospel from the city of Ephesus, where Paul founded a church. John died in the late 90s as the last apostle. He also authored the book of Revelation.
- John was often called the "apostle of love," as love was a major theme in the gospel and in the three epistles, or letters, that he wrote.

The major miracles in John are:
1. Turning water into wine (John 2:1–11)
2. Healing the royal official's son (John 4:46–54)
3. Healing the invalid at Bethsaida (John 5:1–9)
4. Feeding the five thousand (John 6:1–14)
5. Walking on the sea (John 6:15–21)
6. Restoring sight to a blind man (John 9:1–41)
7. Raising Lazarus (John 11:1–44)
8. Catching the 153 fish (John 21:1–14)

John also highlighted who Jesus is by recording the seven "I ams."
1. I am the bread of life.   John 6:35
2. I am the light of the world.   John 8:12
3. I am the gate.   John 10:7, 9
4. I am the good shepherd.   John 10:11, 14
5. I am the resurrection and the life.   John 11:25
6. I am the way and the truth and the life.   John 14:6
7. I am the true vine.   John 15:1, 5

- John recorded no parables in his Gospel.

THE PRESENTATION OF JESUS—JOHN 1–16

John brought Jesus into the first chapter of his book without recording His birth or early years. He went straight to John the Baptist's ministry that preceded Jesus' ministry. John gave insight into Jesus' callings of the disciples. This includes Nathaniel's wisecracking question when told where Jesus was from: "Nazareth! Can anything good come from there?" (John 1:46).

Jesus' encounter with the Samaritan woman at the well explains the heart of worship. Since the Samaritans worshiped at Mount Gerizim and the Jews worshiped in Jerusalem, Jesus told of the coming day when worship would not be "location driven" but rather "spirit driven."

Chapter 11, right before Jesus enters Jerusalem for the last week, gives a foreshadowing of what is to come. By raising Lazarus from the grave, Jesus proved that He had power over death, and that those who believe in Him would never die.

THE INTERCESSION OF JESUS—JOHN 17
Jesus prayed for Himself, for His disciples, and for all future believers in this remarkable prayer. This High Priestly prayer reveals the passionate heart of Jesus toward all of us who believe.

THE CRUCIFIXION OF JESUS—JOHN 18–19:42
John takes the reader through the illegal Jewish trials and civil trials before the cross. After the brutal Roman cross, Jesus, the Lamb of God, died. John gives us a list of those who remained at the cross with Him: Mary, the mother of Jesus; His aunt; Mary, wife of Clopas; and Mary Magdalene. Jesus gave John the charge to take care of His mother.

THE RESURRECTION OF JESUS—JOHN 20–21
After the victory cry from the empty tomb, Jesus appeared to the disciples. Mary Magdalene was the first person to discover the miraculous resurrection. John concluded that all the books in the world could not contain all that Jesus did.

Acts of the Apostles
The Book of the Holy Spirit

OUTLINE
1. The Church in Jerusalem (1–8:3)
2. The Church in Judea and Samaria (8:4–12:25)
3. The Church Goes to the Ends of the Earth (13–28)

INTRODUCTION

Acts of the Apostles is the account of the Holy Spirit's activity through the first church. The church began in Jerusalem, and the apostles, who were now filled with the Holy Spirit, took the gospel to the ends of the earth. This book is a missionary manual for believers. God has saved us, His church, from our sins. Therefore, we are the "community of the redeemed." We are saved and set free. But we have a mission to accomplish, so we are also the "redeeming community." The book of Acts is an exciting journey, and the two primary leaders were two apostles: Peter and Paul. The theme verse is found in 1:8, *"But you will receive power when the Holy Spirit comes on you; and you will be my witnesses in Jerusalem, and in all Judea and Samaria, and to the ends of the earth."*

FAST FACTS

- The book was written by Luke between AD 63 and 70.
- The church's birth and explosive growth is the subject.
- As the men and women of God took the gospel of Jesus Christ to the world, there was always a reaction. Often, people were saved from their sins, yet there was considerable opposition and persecution.
- Acts reminds us that we are all missionaries, and we are each responsible to reach the area of the world that we have been placed in.

THE CHURCH IN JERUSALEM—ACTS 1–8:3

The book begins with the risen Lord Jesus giving final instructions to the apostles. He appeared to believers over a period of forty days for two reasons:

1. To convince them He was alive
2. To teach them about the kingdom of God

The disciples asked Jesus if the kingdom was to come immediately. Jesus told them not to be concerned with that but to take the gospel to the lost. The Holy Spirit would come when Jesus departed, He said. Jesus ascended to heaven from the Mount of Olives.

In Acts 2, the promised Holy Spirit did arrive in power, and the believers spoke in new tongues that they had never heard before. These were real languages; and since Jerusalem was filled with foreigners, the grace of God was declared to them in their own language. Peter summarized the event with a powerful sermon, and a great outpouring began in Jerusalem. Miracles occurred regularly, and the church was added to daily.

As needs arose in the church, deacons were appointed to meet them so the apostles might concentrate on prayer and the ministry of the Word. Stephen arose as a man of faith, full of the Holy Spirit, and served as one of the first deacons. Stephen conflicted with the religious leaders of Jerusalem and was put on trial for it. He preached a sermon that brought the Old Testament and New Testament together, and the leaders reacted violently and killed him. Persecution broke out, and the church began to leave Jerusalem.

THE CHURCH IN JUDEA AND SAMARIA—ACTS 8:4–12:25

Peter and Philip began to take the gospel to the Gentiles. In chapter 10, God gave Peter a vision that confirmed that now was the time to go to the Gentiles with the Word of God. Peter faced a dilemma in that the Gentiles were not circumcised, as the Jews were, and this brought the two groups into conflict. Peter told his Gentile audience of the miraculous vision of God that he had concerning the Gentiles, and that God had granted them repentance now. The stage was set to take the gospel to the world.

THE CHURCH GOES TO THE ENDS OF THE EARTH—ACTS 13–28

Earlier, Paul had been converted from a strict Judaism that led him to the killing of Christians. He had opposed Christianity so vigorously that he actually approved of the stoning of Stephen with great joy. After Paul's Damascus Road conversion, God was now raising him up to take the gospel to the Gentiles. God allowed Paul to suffer much along the way, and eventually he died a martyr's death.

Paul took the gospel to Asia and all the way to Europe. He set sail in three missionary journeys with Barnabas and John Mark and then later with Silas and Luke. In Acts 15, the issue of Gentiles within the church was settled once and for all.

Paul was the greatest instrument that God used in the first century to spread the gospel. He spoke to thousands and brought the gospel to pagan Rome. Paul accomplished an enormous amount of work for God. He planted churches wherever he went and wrote thirteen epistles. His contribution to our faith cannot be overestimated. He wrote almost half of the number of the books of the New Testament. He explained important doctrinal truths, as in Romans. He took the gospel to the world. All of this he accomplished in the power of the Spirit of God while undergoing persecution and serving numerous jail sentences. The church faithfully proclaimed Christ to the world, and that chain of faithfulness has never been broken; our faith in Christ is proof of that.

Romans
The Book of Justification

OUTLINE
1. Righteousness Explained (1–11)
2. Righteousness Lived (12–16)

INTRODUCTION

The book of Romans is the first epistle of the New Testament. An epistle is a letter, and Paul penned this one from Corinth while on a missionary journey there. Paul realized the importance of strategic frontline churches, as the Roman church was situated in the heart of the pagan empire of Rome. The Romans were polytheistic, meaning they believed and honored many gods. Rome was the world's superpower for centuries. The church, however, had been called out of their pagan surroundings to follow the Lord Jesus Christ.

The book covers in depth the wonderful doctrine of justification. Justification is the act of forgiveness that allows a clean standing before our righteous God. It was accomplished on the cross by Jesus Christ. Therefore, the theme of the book is the righteousness of God and how we can be justified before Him.

FAST FACTS
- Paul wrote Romans in AD 57 or 58.
- Paul was martyred in Rome, as was the apostle Peter.
- Before his final journey to Rome, Paul reflected on his missionary career and summarized it doctrinally for us.
- Romans is the most in-depth study of salvation in all of scripture. Major subjects of salvation are discussed and developed for us. A few of them are:
  - Sin (Romans 3:9–20)
  - Justification (Romans 3:24)

- > Propitiation (Romans 3:25)
- > Election of Israel (Romans 9:11)
- > Spiritual Gifts (Romans 12)
- This book is the explanation of our faith and vital for the believer to understand.

RIGHTEOUSNESS EXPLAINED—ROMANS 1–11

Paul begins Romans with a greeting that would become the standard for his epistles—"Paul, a servant of Jesus Christ" (1:1). He also would greet the believers to whom the book was written with the phrase "grace and peace" (1:7). The theme is found in Romans 1:16–17. "The righteousness of God . . . a righteousness that is by faith" is the thrust of the book. In chapter 1, the apostle wrote that no one is excused from condemnation for their sin because God has revealed Himself in nature, and it has been made plain to all. Even if the gospel has not reached someone, that person can still see God in creation and cry out to Him to reveal Himself to him or her. God will always answer this cry from the heart. Unfortunately, many people of Paul's day turned to idolatry instead.

In chapter 3, Paul exposed all of us as unrighteous. "For all of us have sinned and fall short of the glory of God" (v. 23). Since Adam and Eve fell to sin, the entire human race has also. Abraham, the first patriarch, "believed God, and it was credited to him as righteousness" (4:3). It is faith that brings justification to us as sinners. When we believe in faith that Jesus is Savior and repent of our sins, we are justified and receive grace. Grace is what saves us. Faith is what opens salvation to us. Justification is the result that we can enjoy because of it.

Romans 8 boldly declares a right relationship with God that begins at salvation and brings us to face acceptance before God. Verse 1 says *"there is now no condemnation for those who are in Christ Jesus."* Paul's description of the exalted life in Christ is the theme of chapter 8. It is a powerful chapter. Chapters 9–11 describe the grief that Paul felt concerning his fellow Jews. He wanted them to come to Christ so intensely that he wished he could take their place in hell for them. What passion to see the lost saved! Paul also told us that the church does not replace Israel, for God's covenant with them in Genesis 12 is still in effect.

RIGHTEOUSNESS LIVED—ROMANS 12-16

Paul begins this section with a plea to live life right before God. Since we have recovered all of these blessings, it ought to change the way we live. Paul tells us how in chapters 12-16. We are now God's family, the church, and we should live to honor Him. In chapter 13 he informs us that we must respect government and its leaders. In chapter 14, Paul reminds us that each of us will give an account before the Lord. That ought to be all the motivation needed to live daily for God. His only testimony was, *"For I am not ashamed of the gospel, because it is the power of God that brings salvation to everyone who believes: first to the Jew, then to the Gentile. For in the gospel the righteousness of God is revealed—a righteousness that is by faith from first to last, just as it is written: 'The righteous will live by faith.'"* (Romans 1:16-17)

1 Corinthians
The Book of Correction

> **OUTLINE**
> 1. Division in the Church (1–4)
> 2. Sin in the Church (5–6)
> 3. Problems in the Church (7–16)

INTRODUCTION

Corinth was a port city between the Aegean and Adriatic Seas. Since it was located strategically in Asia, it became a center of commerce. Paul planted a church on his second missionary journey there. The city was famous for its sinful ways. With a stadium that held twenty thousand people and the temple of Aphrodite, with its one thousand prostitutes, evil was all over the city.

To be "Corinthianized" meant to be made immoral. Yet, in the midst of this atmosphere, the church existed and was poised to make a difference. Yet they fell into sin. Paul wrote to answer questions the church faced because of its worldliness.

FAST FACTS

- Paul wrote this book in AD 56 to strongly rebuke the believers who were caught up in sin.
- Paul wrote this letter from Ephesus.
- The Lord's Supper, marriage, divorce, spiritual gifts, and what true love is are all covered in 1 Corinthians. Paul largely wrote this book out of great spiritual concern over the irregular behavior of the church. He also wanted to answer the many questions that the believers had.
- The book is very practical and includes subjects that are still important in any church today.

DIVISION IN THE CHURCH—1 CORINTHIANS 1–4

Despite all of the believers' sins and difficulty in their fellowship, Paul called them "sanctified" in 1:2. *Sanctified* means "set apart" for God, but the Corinthians seemed far from it. Yet, their position in Christ made them sanctified before the Lord, and now it was time for their practices to live up to it.

The division within the church was seen in their selfish claims to follow Paul or Apollos or Cephas. But Paul affirmed that only Christ matters. Sure, Paul planted and Apollos watered, but God is the one who caused the growth. Since the divisions were so prevalent, the believers remained in a state of infancy.

SIN IN THE CHURCH—1 CORINTHIANS 5–6

The gravity of the situation in Corinth was extreme, as there was even incest in the church. There were also numerous lawsuits between believers. Paul says this should not be and that we should rather be wronged than tarnish the name of Christ. Moral problems were growing, too. Paul denounced immorality, homosexuality, and other sensual sins. Paul said that as believers we should not be mastered by anything, except for Christ.

PROBLEMS IN THE CHURCH—1 CORINTHIANS 7–16

The bulk of the book is concerned with the various problems that the church was experiencing. Paul taught that divorce in the church was to be rare, and only in the case of infidelity is remarriage acceptable. Paul also explained about meat offered to idols. He warned about taking the Lord's Supper lightly. Some Christians were actually hoarding the food and wine at the holy meal. The Lord had caused some to be sick and some to die as a result of it.

First Corinthians 13 is one of the most loved chapters in the entire Bible. Biblical love is the subject; and like a flower that blooms in spring, the beauty of love is unfolded for all to see in this great chapter. Chapters 12–14 contain a major treatment on spiritual gifts.

The capstone of the book is chapter 15. It is a thorough treatment on the resurrection, which is the bedrock of our faith. Paul closes with a challenge to give financially to the saints in Jerusalem.

2 Corinthians
The Book of Commendation

OUTLINE
1. Commendation of the Church (1–7)
2. Commendation of Paul (8–13)

INTRODUCTION
Paul followed up his first letter to the Corinthians with a second epistle shortly afterward. He wrote to commend the church for its treatment of the immoral brother within the church. Paul also wanted them to know how much he loved them. He also needed to defend his apostleship, which was being questioned by some.

FAST FACTS
- Paul wrote this epistle probably from Philippi about AD 55 or 56.
- Even though there were still problems within the church, Paul was pleased overall with the progress of the fellowship.
- Paul planned to visit the church but had a change in his plans. Titus brought the good news to Paul that the man who had been in sin had repented of immorality, and the church had dealt well with the troubling situation.

COMMENDATION OF THE CHURCH—2 CORINTHIANS 1–7
In chapter 1, Paul related how suffering softens us up to those who are suffering. God allows us to go way past our limit of endurance so that we might trust Him more. In chapter 2, Paul reminded the believers to not be too excessive in their punishment of the moral offender within the church. The Corinthians were Paul's letters written on his heart and read by everyone. Change is a part of the Christian life; and when God produces it, it is called transformation. Paul aimed the believers at this and underscored it with the coming judgment seat of Christ. "For we must all appear before the judgment

seat of Christ" are words that ought to motivate us on a daily basis (5:10). It is the love of Christ that compels us to love and do good deeds. Paul closed the section with a commendation for the believers' repentance.

COMMENDATION OF PAUL—2 CORINTHIANS 8-13

Chapters 8 and 9 are the New Testament's premier passage on giving. God teaches that there ought to be joy in our giving. If we give generously to God, God gives generously to us.

Chapter 10 gives great insight into the spiritual warfare that constantly goes on around us. We have divine power to demolish strongholds through the power of God.

In chapter 12, Paul gives us a glimpse of how difficult his life was. He suffered beatings and imprisonment, and faced death continually. With Godly boasting, he told of his vision as he was caught up to the very presence of God. To keep Paul humble, God gave him a "thorn" in his flesh. (12:7). Possibly, that "thorn" was deteriorating eyesight.

Paul ended his letter to the Corinthians with the admonition to examine themselves to see if they were in the faith or not. Even though the Corinthian church still had its problems, they had come a long way in their faith.

Galatians
The Book of Freedom

 **OUTLINE**
1. Our Position in Christ (1–3)
2. Our Practice in Christ (4–6)

INTRODUCTION
Paul wrote the Epistle of Galatians to a group of churches in Asia Minor. The book is about Christian liberty. The doctrine of justification by faith is emphasized because it is the foundation on which our freedom stands. Paul also wrote to stop the legalistic influence of the Jewish group called the Judaizers. They advocated a "works" salvation that demanded circumcision.

FAST FACTS
- Paul wrote Galatians between AD 49 and 55. It was his first epistle.
- Salvation by grace is the centerpiece of our faith, and the early church struggled with this concept. The question is this: "Does grace stand alone?" The legalistic believers claimed that grace alone could not save a person from condemnation.
- Ironically, Paul wrote this letter on freedom from jail. He was Christ's ambassador in chains.

OUR POSITION IN CHRIST—GALATIANS 1–3
Many of the Galatians had abandoned the gospel of grace and were now espousing another gospel. Paul told the believers of his previous life, in which he persecuted the church and tried to destroy it. But God had called Paul to salvation. In fact, He had set him apart for the preaching of the gospel from birth. If Paul could be forgiven of his great sins and could have a secure position in Christ, so could anyone.

Paul said that the Galatians had not received the Spirit of God by the law, so why would they try to grow in their faith by the law?

OUR PRACTICE IN CHRIST—GALATIANS 4–6

Paul told the Galatians to live by the Spirit of God and not by their sinful nature. It ought to be obvious when we are living by our flesh. Immorality, envy, drunkenness, jealousy, idolatry, and several other sins are named. The fruit of the Spirit is what will be manifested if we allow the Holy Spirit to fill us. This inner transformation is one of the most powerful ways that we can demonstrate Jesus' living in us. Galatians 5:22–23 says, *"But the fruit of the Spirit is love, joy, peace, forbearance, kindness, goodness, faithfulness, gentleness and self-control. Against such things there is no law."*

Paul closes with what to do when someone is caught in sin. Restoration is the goal; and if sin continues, the believers will reap what they sow. Finally, the apostle said that he would only boast in the cross of Christ. It is the cross of death that bought our life of freedom.

Ephesians
The Book of the Body of Christ

OUTLINE
1. Our Possessions (1–3)
2. Our Practice (4–6)

INTRODUCTION

Ephesians is an epistle in a group called the Prison Epistles. Philippians, Colossians, and Philemon are also included in the group that Paul wrote during his Roman imprisonment. A church began in the city of Ephesus on Paul's second missionary journey. The city was famous for the temple of Diana, the pagan fertility goddess. The city was a major center for commerce, religion, and politics. The church in Ephesus was founded by Paul, pastored by Timothy, and later preached in by the apostle John.

FAST FACTS

- Paul wrote the book as a letter to be sent to the churches in the region.
- It was written while Paul spent two years in his first Roman imprisonment in AD 61.
- The theme of the book is the body of Christ and what God invested in her from eternity past.

OUR POSSESSIONS—EPHESIANS 1–3

The believer is blessed with every spiritual blessing in Jesus Christ. Our salvation is secure since we were sealed in the Holy Spirit at the time of our salvation. The apostle had prayed continually since he heard of the newfound church so that they might have a spirit of wisdom and revelation. This would ensure that they would know Christ better and more fully.

We were once dead in our sins, but now, as believers, we have been made alive in Christ. One of the benefits of salvation is that we are "one" in the

Lord. Jew and Gentile both have access to God, and there is no wall of separation between us.

OUR PRACTICE—EPHESIANS 4-6

As Paul wrote from prison, he urged believers to live a life worthy of our calling. Chapters 1–3 are what we should know. Chapters 4–6 are what we should do. One of the ways we can do our duty is by exercising our spiritual gifts. We will build the body of Christ, and we will reach our maximum effectiveness if this happens.

If we are filled with the Spirit, we will have right relationships, whether in the home or at work. The most complete section on spiritual warfare in the New Testament is the subject of chapter 6. We must put on the full armor of God to defeat Satan. He has a scheme to make us fall into sin. But God has called us to stand against the devil's attacks, and Paul repeated this admonition four times in the passage.

Philippians
The Book of Joy

OUTLINE
1. Joy in Suffering and Serving (1–2)
2. Joy in Daily Living (3–4)

INTRODUCTION

This little four-chapter epistle from Paul is a powerhouse full of wisdom for living! The church in Philippi was founded by Paul on his second missionary journey. He wrote this letter from jail to the first church that he established in Europe. This was a strategic city in the Roman Empire and was named after King Philip of Macedonia. The church loved Paul and had sent at least two gifts with Epaphroditus to the aging apostle. Philippians is Paul's thank-you note to the church.

FAST FACTS

- Paul was either in Rome or Caesarea, Israel, when he wrote this letter.
- This letter is one of Paul's later epistles. He only lived a few more years after he penned the letter.
- It was written in AD 63.
- Paul used the terms "joy" and "rejoice" several times throughout the four-chapter book.

JOY IN SUFFERING AND SERVING—PHILIPPIANS 1–2

Paul had been imprisoned for Christ's sake. He wanted the believers in Philippi to know that even in the midst of trials, God's plan for them was right on schedule. God had begun a good work in them and would finish it. Paul rejoiced in his prison chains because it encouraged other brothers and sisters in Christ. The goal, whatever the situation, was for believers to live in a worthy manner of the gospel.

Humility is the attitude that the believer should adopt. Philippians 2:6–11 says that Jesus, "who, being in very nature God, did not consider equality with God something to be used to his own advantage; rather, he made himself nothing by taking the very nature of a servant, being made in human likeness. And being found in appearance as a man, he humbled himself by becoming obedient to death—even death on a cross! Therefore God exalted him to the highest place and gave him the name that is above every name, that at the name of Jesus every knee should bow, in heaven and on earth and under the earth, and every tongue acknowledge that Jesus Christ is Lord, to the glory of God the Father."

This passage is the heart of the epistle. Jesus emptied Himself and took the form of a bondservant. Jesus, of course, was still God, but humbled Himself to take the position of a common servant. This ought to deeply affect our attitude in life.

JOY IN OUR DAILY LIVING—PHILIPPIANS 3–4

The apostle was willing to say everything was trash compared to knowing Jesus. His goal was to know Christ and share in His sufferings and death. He also wanted to know the power of His resurrection. Paul, like a runner, forgot his past and pressed on to the glorious future of freedom.

Chapter 4 has given believers comfort and strength in the midst of adversity for centuries. Don't be anxious! The peace of God will guard your hearts and minds. Paul reminds us that the key to realizing this is:
- maintaining right relationships   Philippians 4:2
- praying about everything   Philippians 4:6
- thinking on the right things   Philippians 4:8–9

Only God can give us real joy in the midst of difficulty. Paul, of course, knew this writing from a jail. Even in chains he was filled to overflowing with the joy of the Lord.

Colossians

The Book of our Completeness in Christ

OUTLINE
1. Christ's Accomplishments (1–2)
2. Our Response (3–5)

INTRODUCTION

Paul wrote to the church in Colossae this small but important epistle. He desired to teach some practical theology to the believers there. Since the city was a major center for trade, the culture had many influences. Unfortunately, they created some confusion in the church as the believers sought to integrate Oriental mysticism and Jewish legalism. Greek philosophy also permeated the church, and so Paul took the believers back to the basics of their faith to prove the sufficiency of Christ.

FAST FACTS

- Paul wrote this letter in AD 61.
- Paul also wrote this epistle from jail.
- Epaphras played the most primary role in evangelizing the area and in planting the church.
- Paul was adamant in battling the false teachings of the day. Those teachings were incompatible with the church. Tychicus was the deliverer of the letter.

CHRIST'S ACCOMPLISHMENTS—COLOSSIANS 1–2

The believers surrounding Paul had a fervent mind-set of prayer for the Colossians and their spiritual growth. And they would grow if they were filled with the knowledge of Jesus. So will we. Jesus rescued us from the dominion of darkness and brought us into the glorious kingdom of light.

In our sin we were enemies of Christ; now, amazingly we share in a great inheritance because of His reconciliation on the cross for us.

Paul warned the Colossians about believers judging them on externals alone. The old Jewish feasts were no longer required of the believers. Angel worship was strictly forbidden.

OUR RESPONSE—COLOSSIANS 3-4

Our true destiny is in heaven, and our minds should be adjusted to live in the light of this. For us, as for the Colossians, this calls for radical dealings with sin. We are to put to death the deeds of the flesh. God's wrath will judge the earth because of these deeds, so why as a believer should we be caught up in them? If we truly adjust our focus to heaven, then our work, relationships, and passion for Christ should reflect this.

Paul closed the letter with personal remarks concerning other believers and his fellow prisoners.

1 Thessalonians
The Book of Encouragement

> **OUTLINE**
> 1. Faith in the Lord (1–3)
> 2. Hope in the Lord (4–5)

INTRODUCTION

1 Thessalonians is also written to a church. Pastoring a church is a difficult job. Paul knew this well; and in the case of the Thessalonians, he received some good news concerning their spiritual progress. This had to be a relief to Paul, their shepherd, since he was away from them. This book brings hope to us in two ways:
1. The church can be effective.
2. Our future will be glorious.

In Acts 17, an account of the church in Thessalonica is recorded. Paul was in the city for three Sabbaths. Amazingly, a church was born and had been weathering the persecution that came its way. Timothy brought the good report to Paul about the church.

FAST FACTS

- The book was written by Paul in AD 51.
- The apostle wrote about the future of the church in chapter 4. The event he described there is the "catching up" of the saints into heaven, known as the rapture. How filled with joy Paul must have been when he heard about the great reputation that the church had in their area.

FAITH IN THE LORD—1 THESSALONIANS 1–3

The believers in Thessalonica were no accident. They had been chosen by God and blessed with hearing the gospel that came to them in the power of the Spirit. Paul reminded them how he reacted to them as a father did to a child, with encouragement and comfort. Three times Paul tried to come to them but was stopped by Satan. The enemy had thrown obstacles in the apostle's way that prevented his return to the city of Thessalonica. Finally, Timothy was able to visit.

HOPE IN THE LORD—1 THESSALONIANS 4-5

The Thessalonians needed to live all the way for God. It was God's will that they should live purely before God. All sexual sin was forbidden. The heathen lived this way, so no believer could adopt this lifestyle and still live a holy life. But living righteously before God brought rewards both present and future. The Thessalonian believers were given this exciting promise:

> *"For the Lord himself will come down from heaven, with a loud command, with the voice of the archangel and with the trumpet call of God, and the dead in Christ will rise first. After that, we who are still alive and are left will be caught up together with them in the clouds to meet the Lord in the air. And so we will be with the Lord forever. Therefore encourage one another with these words"*
> (1 Thessalonians 4:16–18).

The rapture passage pictures the removal of the church from the earth before the coming tribulation. First Thessalonians 5:9 tells us that God has not appointed us for wrath but to receive salvation through Christ. Sinners receive God's wrath, but believers escape it. This gives us great hope for our future.

2 Thessalonians
The Book of Perseverance

OUTLINE
1. The Return of Jesus (1–2)
2. Persevering until Christ's Return (3–4)

INTRODUCTION
Paul wrote this epistle to correct some misunderstanding that the believers had from Paul's previous letter. Some apparently thought that the end of the world was near and were actually just waiting for it. Paul dealt with the Antichrist and the great rebellion that will occur before Christ's return.

FAST FACTS
- The epistle was written by Paul shortly after the first one, in AD 51.
- Many times, Christians are confused about the future and the various judgments of God. Often in our persecution, we can perceive that the end is near when it only seems that way.

THE RETURN OF JESUS—2 THESSALONIANS 1–2
Paul boasted of the Thessalonian believers' perseverance in the midst of their trials. They would be counted worthy of the kingdom of God. Paul told the Thessalonians in chapter 2 that the Antichrist, or man of sin, would one day arrive and lead a great rebellion against God. Daniel 7:25, Matthew 24:15, and Daniel 9:27 also detail this. So, until he was revealed, there was much time to still do the work of God.

PERSEVERING UNTIL CHRIST'S RETURN—2 THESSALONIANS 3–4
Paul assured the believers that God would be the source of strength and protection against Satan. The apostle also urged the idle to settle down and get back to work.

1 Timothy
The Book of Ministry

> OUTLINE
> 1. The Need for Sound Doctrine (1)
> 2. The Need for a Strong Church (2–3)
> 3. The Need for Godly Leaders (4–6)

INTRODUCTION

Now that Paul was in the twilight of his life, he became more and more consumed with the local churches and leadership that he had influenced throughout his ministry. No one was more special to him than Timothy, whom Paul called his "true son in the faith" (1:2). Paul was Timothy's mentor. He had grown up under Paul's ministry; and like Paul, had risked his life for the sake of the gospel. Paul appointed Timothy to be the pastor of the church in Ephesus. This was an enormous challenge since Ephesus was extremely paganistic. Therefore, Paul wrote this pastoral epistle to Timothy, and it is still a textbook for ministers today.

FAST FACTS

- Paul wrote this epistle in AD 63, when Timothy was in the midst of a great spiritual battle.
- Ephesus was the "Sin City" of the day. It was known for its wealth and its sexual promiscuity. This was based around the Temple of Diana, which was the centerpiece of the city. The temple was one of the Seven Wonders of the World. It boasted of 127 columns of marble, each sixty feet high, with the famous idol of Diana in the middle of it. Ephesus was a center for paganism, and the gospel was needed desperately.

THE NEED FOR SOUND DOCTRINE—1 TIMOTHY 1

Paul urged Timothy to stay in Ephesus in order to teach sound doctrine. The church contained certain men that were false teachers, and they were confusing the flock. A major task for Timothy was to correct the damage that had been done to the church through these men.

THE NEED FOR A STRONG CHURCH—1 TIMOTHY 2-3

Beautifully, Paul began this section with what is the most important element in any life-giving New Testament church—prayer. This is so important that Paul broke prayer into four aspects:
1. Requests
2. Prayers
3. Intercession
4. Thanksgiving

Paul taught prayer was to be for everyone, even kings and those in authority, because God wants all men to be saved. Prayer is the key to seeing this happen. If it were up to God, all people would be saved. But He gives all of us the chance to accept or reject His free offer of salvation. Once we choose, God respects our decision.

Men were to be consumed with prayer. Women were to be consumed with good deeds. Overseers, or elders and deacons, were to be godly men; and Paul provided a checklist of qualifications for both leadership positions within the church.

THE NEED FOR GODLY LEADERS—1 TIMOTHY 4-6

Paul, through the Spirit of God, revealed to Timothy that in the last days, apostasy would be widespread. Paul reminded Timothy to be diligent in teaching, rebuking, and correcting the saints. He also gave the young pastor direction concerning widows, elders, and slaves, which were common in the area at the time.

Paul warned Timothy to stay away from the love of money, for it is the root of all sorts of evil. He ended his letter with a final charge to Timothy. It contains these powerful words for any pastor: *"But you, man of God, flee from all this, and pursue righteousness, godliness, faith, love, endurance and gentleness. Fight the good fight of the faith"* (1 Timothy 6:11-12).

New Testament

2 Timothy
The Book of Faithful Ministry

OUTLINE
1. The Character of a Soldier for Christ (1–2)
2. The Charge to a Soldier for Christ (3–4)

INTRODUCTION
Second Timothy is the follow-up to Paul's previous epistle to young Timothy and was written at the close of Paul's life. Timothy had been Paul's disciple, and these words were not only instructive to him but also tender. Paul loved his follower in the faith. Now he was alone and cold in a Roman dungeon, and he asked for a coat to be sent to him. Timothy must have been so eager to see Paul before he went to be with the Lord.

FAST FACTS
- Second Timothy was written by Paul in AD 66, right before he was martyred.
- Paul was in a Roman prison, under the scourge of Emperor Nero. After the burning of Rome, Nero blamed Christians and killed hundreds of saints.

THE CHARACTER OF A SOLDIER FOR CHRIST—2 TIMOTHY 1–2
Timothy had a strong spiritual heritage, a sincere faith, and confirmed spiritual gifts. Paul told him to fan into flame his gift of God. Paul, in chapter 2, gave Timothy the process of discipleship to be reproduced in his church. The process resembled a chain to be unbroken:
- take the things taught to you, and
- entrust then to reliable men,
- who will teach others.

Timothy was not to worry about hardship; but like a good soldier, endure it and please God like a soldier wanting to please his commanding officer. Paul encouraged him to minister as a workman laboring in the Word of God and accurately handling it with care. The key to ministry that God blesses is to have it anchored to the Word of God.

THE CHARGE TO A SOLDIER OF CHRIST—2 TIMOTHY 3-4

In the last days people would be lovers of themselves, Paul warned Timothy. The Word of God is the only antidote.

Second Timothy 3:16-17 says, *"All Scripture is God-breathed and is useful for teaching, rebuking, correcting and training in righteousness, so that the servant of God may be thoroughly equipped for every good work."*

These verses give proof that Scripture is inspired by God, literally breathed out by Him. The Bible is without error and is all we need for ministry, whether it be:
- teaching,
- rebuking,
- correcting, or
- training in righteousness.

Therefore, Paul could give Timothy the charge to preach the Word always. This had been the cornerstone of Paul's ministry, and now he passed this on to Timothy. Paul closed with a godly confidence that he had fought the good fight and finished the race. He was ready to go home and meet Jesus.

New Testament

Titus

The Book of Pastoral Leadership

OUTLINE
1. Leadership in the Church (1)
2. Duties Within the Church (2–3)

INTRODUCTION

Titus was like Timothy—a pastor. Paul had discipled him also and left Titus on the island of Crete to build the leadership team of the new churches. He wanted to encourage Titus in this difficult ministry assignment. The churches needed godly leaders, and Paul stressed how important this was to Pastor Titus.

FAST FACTS

- Paul wrote this pastoral epistle in AD 66.
- Titus was a Gentile who came to Christ through the ministry of Paul. He was there with Paul when the apostle traveled to Jerusalem for the council in Acts 15.

LEADERSHIP IN THE CHURCH—TITUS 1

Paul explained why he had left Titus in Crete to organize the work and appoint elders. The ministry involves administration and leadership. The church will keep on task and be effective if a pastor builds a godly leadership team. Paul gave Titus a list of qualifications for elders. He also gave Titus a must for all ministers—silence the rebellious. Evil spreads quickly in the church, but a good minister will stop it quickly.

DUTIES WITHIN THE CHURCH—TITUS 2–3

Building the flock demands that a pastor teach sound doctrine. "Teach, encourage, and rebuke with authority," Paul told Titus. In chapter 3, Titus was told to pass on the need for the people to be subject to rulers and authorities and to slander no one.

Before Paul closed the epistle with the normal greetings and final messages, he reminded Timothy, "[Jesus] saved us, not because of righteous things we had done, but because of his mercy. He saved us through the washing of rebirth and renewal by the Holy Spirit." These truths were to be stressed to the believers, as they were excellent and profitable for all.

Philemon
The Book of Forgiveness

 OUTLINE
1. A Plea to Philemon (1)

INTRODUCTION

Philemon was the last of the prison epistles written by Paul to a slave owner named Philemon. This book presents a beautiful picture of forgiveness as experienced by a lowly slave.

FAST FACTS

- Paul wrote this in AD 63.
- Philemon was a slave owner in the Colossian church. Slave trading was a common practice in the first century, and the subject of the book was one slave in particular named Onesimus.

A PLEA TO PHILEMON—PHILEMON 1

In the beginning of the short letter, Paul illustrated an important spiritual key. In verse 6, he said that he prayed that Philemon was active in sharing his faith in order that he would have a full understanding of all that we have in Christ. Philemon was a joy to be around and had "refreshed" the hearts of the saints, Paul wrote.

Paul next pleaded with Philemon to forgive Onesimus. Apparently, Onesimus had run away from Philemon, costing him greatly in lost work and extra expenses. In the meantime, though, Onesimus had become a believer. Paul gave us a picture of grace as he asked Philemon to charge anything Onesimus owed to him. He also urged Philemon to welcome Onesimus, upon his return, as he would welcome Paul.

Hebrews
The Book of Christ's Superiority

OUTLINE
1. The Person of Christ (1–4)
2. The Priesthood of Christ (5–10)
3. The Power of Christ (11–13)

INTRODUCTION

This magnificent book is like a rare piece of art that is unsigned. No one other than God Himself knows who wrote this majestic and magnificent book. The list of possible authors is long and includes:
- Paul
- Barnabas
- Apollos
- Silas
- Aquila
- Priscilla

The book was written to Jewish believers who lived in either Italy or Israel. The theme is the superiority of our Savior, Jesus Christ. The book is thoroughly Jewish, as seen in its numerous quotations of the Old Testament.

FAST FACTS
- The book was written between 60 AD–70 AD.
- Since Jerusalem fell in 70 AD, it would seem that the writer would have mentioned that catastrophic event had it already happened, especially to a Hebrew audience.
- Christ's preeminence is skillfully woven throughout the whole book!

THE PERSON OF CHRIST—HEBREWS 1–4

Jesus Christ is the exact representation of God. In the past, God spoke to us through the prophets in different ways and in different times, but now He speaks to us in Jesus Christ. Jesus is superior to all angels, even though they are important messengers of God. Christ is superior to Moses, although he was a faithful servant in God's house. But in Moses' days there were people who missed out on God's blessings through unbelief. The writer warned against repeating this big mistake.

God's Word is alive! It is what can take a person apart and judge his or her very thoughts. The writer of Hebrews made this point loudly and clearly in this section.

THE PRIESTHOOD OF CHRIST—HEBREWS 5-10

Jesus, our High Priest, is superior to all other priests—even to Melchizedek, the first priest mentioned in the Bible. The priesthood could not bring perfection to the Israelites; only Jesus could save them.

The priest in the Old Testament had to sacrifice endlessly. In the Old Testament temple, there was no chair in the entire building because the priest's work was never done. But Jesus was sacrificed once and for all on the cross; and when the sacrifice was completed, He sat down at the right hand of God. Jesus' blood is superior to that of bulls and goats and able to cleanse us from sin forever. The writer of this book reminded the Hebrews to draw near to God now that they had confidence to enter the Most Holy Place by the blood of Jesus.

THE POWER OF CHRIST—HEBREWS 11-13

Hebrews 11 is God's dynamic Hall of Faith. The saints of the Old Testament are listed one by one according to their great acts of faith. The writer encouraged the readers to live accordingly since such a great cloud of witnesses surrounds us. The only way to do this is to be like a runner in a race—by throwing off anything that slows us up, like sin, and by fixing our eyes on Jesus, as a runner focuses on the finish line. The letter ends with an admonition to have a pure marriage, a respect for leaders, and a plea for prayer. Hebrews 13:20-21 says: "May the God of peace, who through the blood of the eternal covenant brought back from the dead our Lord Jesus, that great Shepherd of the sheep, equip you with everything good for doing his will, and may he work in us what is pleasing to him, through Jesus Christ, to whom be glory for ever and ever. Amen."

James
The Book of Proof

OUTLINE
1. Trials and Doing the Word (1–2)
2. The Tongue, the Devil, and Prayer (3–5)

INTRODUCTION

James is a general epistle written to the church universal and not just one specific church. Its author, James, was the half brother of Jesus, born of the same mother. (Since Jesus was born of a virgin and was not the physical son of Joseph, He and James could only be half brothers.) James is the earliest—and the most practical—book of the New Testament. It does not disagree with Paul's writings about faith even though it stresses works. James looks at our life in Christ from what the results should look like.

FAST FACTS

- The book was written by James in 45 AD.
- James wrote less about theology and more about the practicals of our faith.
- James gives us direction in key subjects, such as trials, the tongue, prayer for the sick, and equality within the body.

TRIALS AND DOING THE WORD—JAMES 1–2

James starts with a surprising verse that tells the readers when under trials to have joy. The joy comes in knowing that trials set in motion are a process that leads to maturity. God does not tempt us with sin but does allow trials for our benefit.

According to James, pure religion is one that can control the mouth and also has a heart to help widows and orphans. In other words, James says, "show me your faith, rather than telling me about it."

THE TONGUE, THE DEVIL, AND PRAYER—JAMES 3-5

The tongue is a small part of our body, yet so destructive. It is like a forest fire that starts small but then sets the forest on fire. How can we praise God and curse men at the same time? If believers will guard their tongues and resist the devil, James taught, they will be on their way to maturity.

James was known as "Camel Knees" in the first century because of scars and bumps on his knees due to long hours of daily prayer. He was the model of a true prayer warrior. He closed his short book with an admonition for sick believers to call the elders of the church for prayer and the anointing of oil. If the prayer was offered in faith, he said, healing would occur.

1 Peter
The Book of Grace

OUTLINE
1. Grace in Growing (1–2:10)
2. Grace in Relationships (2:11- 3:12)
3. Grace in Suffering and Service (3:13–5:14)

INTRODUCTION

In 1 Peter, the apostle Peter elevated the Christian life to a new height. Despite the suffering they were undergoing, being in Christ brought many blessings as well. Peter knew this since he had one of the biggest collapses ever recorded in Scripture. At a time when his Savior needed him most, Peter had denied the Lord; not once but three times. Remarkably, Peter experienced God's grace and was forgiven of his failure in Luke 22:54–62. In Acts, we find Peter as a mighty preacher and the leader of the first church.

FAST FACTS

- Peter wrote his epistle from Rome in 63 AD.
- He referred to Rome as "Babylon," which was symbolic for the city because of its overt evil.
- Peter stayed in Rome the last decade of his life, and he was martyred in 67 AD. His death was a difficult one, as Christ had prophesied in John 21:18–19. Peter was crucified in Rome, upside down.
- Perhaps no other disciple ever experienced as much grace as Peter. He reflected this in the theme of his book in 5:12 as he talked about "the true grace of God."

GRACE IN GROWING—1 PETER 1–2:10

Peter wrote to God's elect, who were strangers in the world and scattered around. God's great mercy has given us a new birth and a living hope through the resurrection of Christ. Our salvation is so great in that the prophets of old could see it from afar but never fully realized it. Angels, who are not given a second chance and have an experience devoid of grace, also long to look into what it means.

Peter called the believers to whom he wrote to a life of maturity. He reminded them that they were now the royal priesthood and chosen people who declare the praises of Him who called them out of the darkness into His wonderful light. So are we, and we must never forget it.

GRACE IN RELATIONSHIPS—1 PETER 2:11–3:12

Grace means that we are willing to submit to masters and bosses. It means that husbands are considerate and respectful of their wives. And it means that wives honor their husbands and work on the inside, not just the outside, appearance.

GRACE IN SUFFERING AND SERVICE—1 PETER 3:13–5:14

Peter wrote in a time when persecution was beginning to break out in Rome. He told the believers to not be surprised at their painful trials but to rejoice in them. Persecution brings blessings from God. Peter next turned to the "shepherds," or pastors, and taught them how to lead the flock. Peter, of course, was an expert in this, since he learned from Jesus, the Great Shepherd Himself. Even so, Peter wrote this epistle in a true spirit of humility, as he himself had experienced grace as few people ever had or ever would.

2 Peter

The Book of Growing Faith

OUTLINE
1. Our Faith (1–2)
2. Our Future (3)

INTRODUCTION

The book of 2 Peter was written within a year of Peter's death. Still living in a Roman jail, Peter was soon to finish his life of serving Christ. Peter and Paul were crucified on the same day, church tradition tells us. The apostles were ultimately killed because they were eyewitnesses of the resurrection. Romans held to emperor worship; and to them, the apostles were atheistic.

FAST FACTS

- Peter wrote his last epistle in 66 or 67 AD.
- Peter wrote to build up the body of believers and to counter the destructive heresies in the church.
- He highlighted major themes of importance, such as the transfiguration of Christ, the inspiration of Scripture, and the second coming of Christ.

OUR FAITH—2 PETER 1-2

God's awesome power has given us everything we need to be godly and to grow in our faith. Even though Peter's life was almost over, he committed to remind believers over and over about all the resources that were available to them in Jesus Christ. Peter wanted to refresh them as long as he was alive. He next gave us an important truth about Scripture. In 1:21, he tells us that God moved men by the Holy Spirit in the prophetic gifts. The Scriptures were not from man, but from God. Finally in this section, he compared the fate of false teachers with the angels that fell from heaven.

OUR FUTURE—2 PETER 3

Peter next turned to the last days and to the scoffers that will deny truth and follow their own desires and not God's. They will laugh at the thought of the coming of the Lord. Just as flooding waters in Noah's day destroyed the world, so it will be with fire in the future. The Day of the Lord will come as quickly as a thief, the apostle warned.

1 John
The Book of True Fellowship

OUTLINE
1. A True Fellowship (1–3)
2. A Dynamic Fellowship (4–5)

INTRODUCTION

After Paul, John the apostle wrote the most books in the New Testament, with five. The "son of thunder," as Jesus called him, was without a doubt the closest to Jesus of all the disciples. He was a fisherman by trade. John spent the latter part of his life in Ephesus and died in his nineties.

There was a heresy beginning to permeate the church in John's last days, known as Gnosticism. It stressed knowledge over right living and looked at Scripture as being nonliteral. What further added to the danger was that it claimed that Jesus did not physically rise from the dead. John defeated this erroneous doctrine conclusively in this first epistle.

FAST FACTS
- John wrote this letter in 90 AD.
- He loved the body of Christ, as he affectionately called them "dear children" nine times in his book.
- John characteristically spoke of contrasts, such as light and darkness, and love and hate.
- We are told from history that John preached his last sermon in Ephesus as an old man, barely able to walk. His last words were "love the brethren, love the brethren." John truly was the apostle of love. He was the only apostle that was not martyred.

A TRUE FELLOWSHIP—1 JOHN 1–3

John wrote this book and was filled with joy because of what God was doing in the life of the believers. The classic understanding of forgiveness for the believer is found in 1:9. We do struggle with sin; and if we claim we don't, we are only deceiving ourselves. John next wrote to the church, specifically and individually addressing the fathers, the young men, and the children. "Do not love the world or anything in the world," he cried out to them.

In chapter 3, he reminds us that when Christ appears, we will be like Him. We will be purified and perfect in heaven one day.

A DYNAMIC FELLOWSHIP—1 JOHN 4–5

The flock of believers will often have false believers within it. According to John, we are to test their spirits to determine if they are believers or not. All will know this by their stance on the resurrection. The Gnostics believed Christ could not have risen from the dead physically. John charged that no one who holds this view can be a believer. He also wrote that those who do not love others cannot know God. "We love because he first loved us," he said (4:20). John concluded with the theme of the book, in 5:13—"I write these things to you who believe in the name of the Son of God so that you may know that you have eternal life."

We have the beautiful assurance of knowing that we have eternal life. John went to his grave with this confidence—confidence that he wanted all believers to possess.

2 John
The Book of Follow-Through

 OUTLINE
1. Walking in the Truth

INTRODUCTION
John wrote this short letter to a "lady chosen by God," probably a believer, during his time. Some have held that the phrase "lady chosen by God" is figurative for the church.

FAST FACTS
- The book was written by John about the same time 1 John was, in 90 AD.
- The thrust of the book is that we must obey God and walk in the truth.

WALKING IN THE TRUTH—2 JOHN
John told the chosen lady that he had great joy in knowing that her children were walking in the truth. They were to continue to walk in the truth and watch out for deceivers in the world, equally great advice for believers today.

3 John
The Book of Rebuke

 OUTLINE
1. Godliness Contrasted with Selfishness

INTRODUCTION
This third epistle is a rebuke of a brother in the church named Diotrephes, who was consumed with selfishness. John also commended a man named Gaius for his faithfulness, as well as a man named Demetrius.

FAST FACTS
- This book is personal, as it is addressed to Gaius.
- It was written by John in 90 AD.

GODLINESS CONTRASTED WITH SELFISHNESS
John's joy could have been no greater than when he knew that his spiritual children were walking in the truth (v. 4). Gaius and Demetrius displayed this kind of living. Diotrephes did not, however, and John told them to have nothing to do with him.

Jude
The Book of Apologetics

 OUTLINE
1. Exposing False Teachers (1)

INTRODUCTION
Jude was the brother of James and the half brother of Jesus. He is listed in Matthew 13:55 and Mark 6:3 as a member of Jesus' physical family. This book was written to stop the heresy that was spreading to many New Testament churches.

FAST FACTS
- Jude wrote the letter between 70 and 80 AD.
- He called the believers "to contend for their faith."
- He also attacked the false doctrine of Gnosticism. This heresy allowed every kind of sin to be practiced freely. Gnostics were grace abusers.

EXPOSING FALSE TEACHERS
The saints of God had been given the faith or body of truth once and for all. They were now to fight for it, defend it, and protect it. Jude reminded the believers of the fate of the unbelieving Jews who were delivered from Egypt. Likewise, angels in heaven were judged and cast down into darkness.

He next called the false teachers dreamers. "On the strength of their dreams these ungodly people pollute their own bodies, reject authority and heap abuse on celestial beings," he said (v. 8). Jude went on to deliver a judgment against these heretics in the form of a "woe" (v. 11), as Jesus had done to the Pharisees and other heretics. In the last days, heresy will become more prevalent, but Jesus "is able to keep you from stumbling and to present you before his glorious presence without fault and with great joy" (v. 24).

Revelation

The Book of End Times

> OUTLINE
> 1. What John Saw (1)
> 2. What Is (2–3)
> 3. What Is to Come (4–22)

INTRODUCTION

The book of Revelation is the most misunderstood book in the Bible. Part of the problem is its extensive use of symbolism. The symbols belong to the first century and not the twenty-first; therefore, they are often difficult to decipher. But God promises to bless those who read, hear, and take to heart the words of this powerful book. We are blessed just for merely reading it. Many Christians miss out on blessings intended for them due to their avoidance of this book.

The word "revelation" means "disclosure" or "unveiling." The common title of the book is "The Revelation of John," but this only describes the human writer and to whom the revelation is revealed. The revelation is of Jesus Christ; and He is the center, the theme, and the believer's hope throughout the entire book.

FAST FACTS

- John the apostle is our writer. He wrote this final book of the Bible at the end of his life, in 90 AD, from Patmos.
- Literature that is *apocalyptic* (Greek for "revelation") is normally very pessimistic in nature. Yet, Revelation is optimistic.
- The Messiah is seen in the future, but Revelation presents Jesus Christ as having already come.
- There are four basic ways to interpret Revelation.

1. The Nonliteral or Allegorical Approach: The book is viewed as a message of encouragement to the church but not to be taken literally.
2. The Preterist Approach: The future implications of the book are denied, and Revelation is seen as a historical account of Christianity. The prophecies in the book have been fulfilled already.
3. The Historical Approach: The book is taken at face value as a panorama of history from John's time to the end.
4. The Futurist Approach: The book is seen as largely unfulfilled. This is the most logical view of the book, as seen in the outline.

WHAT JOHN SAW—REVELATION 1

John introduced the book with the built-in blessing in verse 3. An angel was sent to John, and then the vision was revealed. John addressed the book to seven churches that existed in Asia during the time of the writing. Immediately, John takes the reader to the great event of Christ's return. Revelation 1:4–8 says:

John,

To the seven churches in the province of Asia:

Grace and peace to you from him who is, and who was, and who is to come, and from the seven spirits before his throne, and from Jesus Christ, who is the faithful witness, the firstborn from the dead, and the ruler of the kings of the earth.

To him who loves us and has freed us from our sins by his blood, and has made us to be a kingdom and priests to serve his God and Father—to him be glory and power for ever and ever! Amen.

"Look, he is coming with the clouds,"
and "every eye will see him,
even those who pierced him";
and all peoples on earth "will mourn because of him."

So shall it be! Amen.

"I am the Alpha and the Omega," says the Lord God, "who is, and who was, and who is to come, the Almighty."

John was in the Spirit when a trumpet sounded, and a loud voice cried out. Next, he was given a vision of the glorious risen Lord Jesus Christ. He was brilliant, and John fell at His feet as a dead man.

WHAT IS—REVELATION 2–3
John was instructed to write to the seven churches. Each had a unique message from Jesus concerning their spiritual condition. In Scripture, "seven" is God's number. It speaks of His completeness. The number seven is used throughout Revelation:
- seven churches
- seven trumpets
- seven scrolls
- seven seals

The seven churches were actual churches, and they provide for us powerful messages for the church of today.
- Ephesus—the church that lost their first love
- Smyrna—the suffering church
- Pergamum—the false teaching church
- Thyatira—the worldly church
- Sardis—the dead church
- Philadelphia—the faithful church
- Laodicea—the unknown church

WHAT IS TO COME—REVELATION 4–22
Chapter 4 begins the largest section of the book and is yet to be fulfilled. A detailed analysis is provided:

The Tribulation (Revelation 4:1–19:21)
1. **The Throne of God (Revelation 4:1–11).** The setting is heaven, and John pictured the glory of it all, living creatures praising God, and the twenty-four elders seated. This, along with chapter 5, forms the background of the action to come. What a privilege John was given, and how it must have comforted those in persecution to have a sneak preview of their future home. Its reason for inclusion in the book, of course, was to provide hope for the seven churches. It appears that the church is out of the picture, having been raptured home with the Lord.

2. **The Scroll (Revelation 5:1–14).** The prejudgment search for one worthy to break the seal and open the letter ends with Christ. He is the only one fit, and the picture of Him in control of the coming judgments provides encouragement for those who are His.

3. **The Seal Judgments (Revelation 6:1–17).** The beginning of God's wrath is to be poured out, and, of course, if any type of literal meaning is to be understood, these must all be coming in the future.

4. **The Redeemed (Revelation 7:1–17).** Chapter 7 does not progress after the events of chapter 6 but rather presents an interlude of the two major groups of saints in the tribulation. The 144,000 Jews are from each of the twelve tribes, and these are made secure, or sealed. The point is not if these are the only ones saved but that this number is secured. A multitude of Gentiles would be saved also. By way of encouragement, the seven churches would not have to go through the wrath to obtain salvation.

5. **The Six Trumpet Judgments (Revelation 8:1–9:21).** This section opens with the seventh seal. The trumpets, therefore, do not double back over the seals but lie under the sixth seal; that is, they do not follow the seals but are the seventh seal.

6. **The Little Scroll (Revelation 10:1–11).** John's reception of the little scroll brought the same reaction as did Ezekiel's: it was pleasant to the

taste because of grace, yet bitter at the same time because of the impending judgment.

7. **The Two Witnesses (Revelation 11:1–19).** The two witnesses are probably a return of Moses and Elijah to earth during the height of the tribulation after the temple is rebuilt. God's faithful duo overcomes the beast and his puppet king, the Antichrist, but are martyred and then resurrected in front of all the nations after a completed mission.

8. **War (Revelation 12:1–17)**

9. **The Beast and the False Prophet (Revelation 13:1–18)**

10. **Announcements (Revelation 14:1–20).** In chapters 12–14, there are seven major people:
    1. Woman—Israel
    2. Dragon—Satan
    3. Man child—Christ
    4. Michael—angel
    5. Israel—the remnant of the seed of the woman
    6. Beast—a world dictator
    7. Beast out of the earth—the false prophet

11. **Prelude to the Bowl Judgments (Revelation 15:1–8)**

12. **The Bowl Judgments (Revelation 16:1–21).** These events bring to an end the order of the things that occur leading up to Christ's second coming. They are introduced as the seven last plagues. John allows the reader to relax; the vengeance of God rests.

13. **Babylon the Harlot (Revelation 17:1–18:24).** These chapters are dedicated to the description of the final destruction of Babylon, representing false religion. Babylon's alliance with the apostate church and political powers ruled by Satan will obtain for them a judgment that devastates them completely.

14. **The Second Coming (Revelation 19:1–21).** John marvelously pictured, in vivid, picturesque language, the triumphant Christ calmly returning to the earth. Christ takes control of the chaotic mess that Satan has caused. What a beautiful sight for every believer to behold.

15. **The Millennium (Revelation 20:1–15).** Several events take place during the literal thousand-year reign of Christ, but this section revolves around all the subjects getting what they deserve: Satan is bound and cast into the lake of fire forever, and the sinners are judged according to their works.

16. **The Eternal State (Revelation 21:1–8).** The heavenly city of the New Jerusalem will be the abode of the saints. The glorious description of the believers' home is a final crown to those who were being tortured in the churches in John's day—and to every persecuted believer since.

17. **Closing (Revelation 22:6–21).** John wraps up the Revelation with a return to his normal state again, attaching his name as a testimony. He again warns of the impending judgment and cautions those who might tamper with the contents of the book.

In conclusion, John's purpose of challenging and encouraging the young churches is complete. He has:
- commended and warned;
- revealed Jesus Christ, the head of the church itself, in all His strength and splendor; and
- shown how the seven churches fit in the overall program of God.

If the young churches were intimidated by the external pressure of the times, John gave them every reason to believe that they would survive and be rewarded by the One who walks in their midst. So will we. And those who were on the side of Satan will be dealt with severely in the future and will reap their own condemnation—while we rejoice with Christ forevermore.

Come, Lord Jesus!

ADDITIONAL RESOURCES

Israel Timeline — Old Testament

	Patriarchal Period 2166-1805 BC	Egyptian Sojourn 1805-1446 BC	Conquest 1406-1375 BC	Judges 1375-1050 BC	United Kingdom 1050-930 BC
Major Events	Abraham is born 2166 BC / Joseph dies in Egypt 1805 BC	Moses crosses the Red Sea 1446 BC	Joshua & the Israelites enter the Promise Land 1406 BC	Judges rule Israel 1375 BC	King Saul 1050 BC / King David 1010 BC / King Solomon 970 BC
Books Written During this Period	Job	Genesis, Exodus, Leviticus, Numbers, Deuteronomy	Joshua	Judges, Ruth	1-2 Samuel, 1 Kings, 1 Chronicles, Psalms, Proverbs, Ecclesiastes, Song of Solomon

	Divided Kingdom 930-586 BC	Captivity 586-516 BC	Return 516-432 BC	Silence 400-4 BC
Major Events	Solomon's disobedience splits the Kingdom into: Israel-North Judah-South 930 BC / Assyrian Captivity 722 BC	Babylonian Captivity 586 BC / First Temple destroyed 586 BC / Persian Empire 538-332 BC	Cyrus King of Persia issues decree for exiles to return to Israel 538 BC / Temple rebuilt under Zerubbabel and Ezra 516 BC / Jerusalem walls rebuilt under Nehemiah 444 BC	4 centuries of silence from God / John the Baptist is born 4 BC / Jesus is born 4 BC / Greek (Hellenistic) Empire 332-63 BC / Alexander the Great 336-323 BC
Books Written During this Period	2 Kings, 2 Chronicles, Isaiah, Jeremiah, Lamentations, Hosea, Joel, Amos, Obediah, Jonah, Micah, Nahum, Habakkuk, Zephaniah	Ezekiel, Daniel	Ezra, Nehemiah, Esther, Haggai, Zechariah, Malachi	

Israel Timeline — New Testament to Today

	Jesus & the Apostles 4BC-90 AD	Byzantine Period 324-638 AD	Early Muslim Period 638-1099 AD	Crusader Period 1099-1260 AD
Major Events	Jesus is born 4 BC The Cross and Resurrection 30 AD Apostolic Period 30 AD-90 AD Roman Rule 63 BC-324 AD	Church Council Period Constantinople is the headquarters for the Church	The Great Schism 1054 AD The Church divides into: Western Catholicism & Eastern Orthodoxy	3 crusades launched by Pope Urban II to take Jerusalem back from Muslims and Jews Saladin defeats the Crusaders at the Horns of Hittin in Galilee 1187 AD
Books Written During this Period	All New Testament books are written			

	Mamluk Period 1260-1517 AD	Ottoman Empire 1517 AD	British Mandate 1917-1948 AD	The State of Israel 1948 AD
Major Events	Mamluks (Egyptian Muslim slaves) rule the Middle East	Suleiman rebuilds the walls of Jerusalem 1542 WWI ends Ottoman Empire 1917	Great Britain occupies the Land of Israel for 30 years	Israel becomes a nation May 14, 1948 5 Arab nations attack Israel May 15, 1948

Israel's and Judah's Kings

The United Kingdom

Saul

David

Solomon

The Divided Kingdom

Israel	Judah
Jeroboam - Golden calves	Rehoboam - Evil
Nadab - Evil	Abijah - Sins of Father
Baasha - Evil	Asa - "Wholly Devoted"
Elah - Murdered Drunk	Jehoshaphat - As Asa
Zimri - Suicide	Jehoram - Evil (slew brothers)
Tibni - Omri takes over	Ahaziah - Idolator
Omri - More evil than all	Athaliah - Daughter of Ahab/Jezebel
Ahab - More evil yet	Joash - Idolator/ evil
Ahaziah - Follow sin of Jeroboam	Amaziah - Good, yet some idolatry
Joram (Jehoram) - Follows sin of Jeroboam	Uzziah - Good
Jehu - Wipes out Ahab's lot, sins also	Jotham - Good
Jehoahaz - Calf worship	Ahaz - Evil, divination, etc.
Jehoash - Calf worship	Hezekiah - Good, removes idols (Best King)
Jeroboam II - Calf worship	Manasseh - Evil, rebuilds altars
Zechariah - Calf worship	Amon - Evil, serves idols
Shallum - Slew Zechariah	Josiah - Good
Menahem - Slew Shallum	Jehoahaz - Evil, as his father
Pekahiah - Calf worship	Jehoiakim - Evil, as his father
Pekah - Slew Pekahiah	Jehoichin - Evil, as his father
Hoshea - More evil than all, divination, etc	Zedekiah - Evil, as his father
The Kingdom ends with Israel being sent by God to the Assyrian Captivity 722 BC	The Kingdom ends with Judah being sent to the Babylonian Captivity 586 BC

ADDITIONAL RESOURCES

God's Concern for the Nations
Ray Hutchison, SIM

Person, People or Event	Reference	Approximate Date
Right after Adam and Eve sin, God promises to send the seed of the woman who will crush the head of the serpent.	Genesis 3:15	
God promises that He would never again destroy the world by a flood.	Genesis 9:8-17	The flood may have taken place less than 500 years before Abram was born around 2166 BC - Calculate the years between Shem and Abram in Genesis 11:10-26
All the nations will be blessed through Abraham and his descendants.	Genesis 12:1-3; 18:17-18; 22:15-18	2,090 BC
Melchizedek, a worshipper of God, serves as a priest.	Genesis 14:18-21	2,080 BC
Even though Ishmael is not the promised child, through which God would bless the nations, God promises to bless him and make him fruitful.	Genesis 17:19-20	2,065 BC
All the nations will be blessed through Jacob and his descendants.	Genesis 26:4; 28:12-14	2,000 BC
God has mercy on Rahab (a Canaanite) and her family.	Joshua 2:1-7; 6:23-25	1,400 BC
God includes Ruth (a Moabite - a descendant of Lot's older daughter) in the family line of Jesus.	Book of Ruth	1,175 BC
The Psalmist (perhaps David) calls for God to bring salvation and blessing to the nations.	Psalm 67:1-7	1,000 BC
The Psalmist (around David's time) declares God's salvation and glory among the nations.	Psalm 96:1-3	975 BC
Solomon expresses God's acceptance of God worshippers from among the nations.	1 Kings 8:41-43	966 BC
Through Elijah, God has compassion for the widow of Zarephath (a Canaanite).	1 Kings 17:9-24	860 BC
Through Elisha, God has compassion on Naaman the Syrian.	2 Kings 5:1-27	835 BC
Through Jonah, God has compassion on the people of Nineveh (Assyrians).	Book of Jonah	760 BC
Through Isaiah, God promises that Egypt and Assyria will be blessed right along with Israel.	Isaiah 19:23-25	730 BC
Through the Servant (Messiah), God promises to bring justice to the nations.	Isaiah 42:1	730 BC

God's Concern for the Nations (continued)
Ray Hutchison, SIM

Person, People or Event	Reference	Approximate Date
Through Isaiah, God promises that the scattered people of Israel will declare God's glory among the nations.	Isaiah 66:18-19	710 BC
Micah declares that in the last days the nations will stream to the mountain of God to praise God.	Micah 4:1-3	700 BC
King Nebuchadnezzar recognizes that the Most High God performed wonders for him.	Daniel 4:1-3	575 BC
Through Zechariah, God promises that people from all nations will seek to know the Lord.	Zechariah 8:20-23	520-518 BC
Through Malachi, God proclaims that His name will be great among the nations.	Malachi 1:11	410 BC
Through Simeon, God declares that the newborn Jesus is a light to the nations.	Luke 2:28-32	4 BC
Because God loves the world He gives His Son, Jesus, so that those who believe in Him will not perish but have eternal life.	John 3:16-18	29-31 AD
Jesus brings salvation to the Samaritans.	John 4:4-42	29-31 AD
Jesus demonstrates God's acceptance of the Gentiles by healing the daughter of the Canaanite woman from demon possession.	Matthew 15:21-28	29-31 AD
Jesus promises that the gospel would be preached to the whole world as a testimony to all nations before the end would come.	Matthew 24:14	30-32 AD
Jesus commands His disciple to preach repentance and make disciples of all nations starting in Jerusalem and serving as His disciples to the ends of the earth.	Matthew 28:18-20; Luke 24:45-48; Acts 1:8	30-32 AD
God prepares the Ethiopian official to hear the gospel and sends Philip to preach it.	Acts 8:26-39	32 AD
Paul is the apostle to the Jews and to the Gentiles.	Acts 9:15-16	33-34 AD
God shows Peter through the conversations of Cornelius that He is interested in reaching the Gentiles.	Acts 10:9-48	37-39 AD
God establishes a church in Antioch, made up of Jews and Gentiles, to send out Paul and Barnabas.	Acts 11:19-30; 13:1-3	45 AD
It is Paul's ambition to preach the gospel where it had not been preached.	Romans 15:17-21	58 AD
John has a vision of the Lamb taking the scroll from God as a representation of purchasing men for God from every tribe and tongue and people and nation.	Revelation 5:6-12	90+ AD

Prophecies About the Coming of Jesus the Messiah
Ray Hutchison, SIM

Prophecy Content	Prophecy Made	Prophecy Fulfilled
God would send someone who would crush Satan's head	Genesis 3:14-15	Luke 2:5-7, 8-11; Galatians 4:4
He would come through Abraham's family and bless the world	Genesis 12:2	Matthew 1:1
He would come through the family of Isaac	Genesis 17:19	Matthew 1:2; Luke 3:34
He would come through the family of Jacob	Genesis 28:10-15; Numbers 24:17	Matthew 1:2; Luke 3:34
He would come from the family of Judah	Genesis 49:10	Matthew 1:2-3; Luke 3:33
He would come through the family of David	2 Samuel 7:8-16; 1 Chronicles 17:7-14	Matthew 1:1; Revelation 22:16
He would be born of a virgin	Isaiah 7:14	Matthew 1:18-23
He would be born in Bethlehem Ephrathah	Micah 5:2	Matthew 2:3-6; Luke 2:4-7
Mothers would cry over their sons killed in Bethlehem	Jeremiah 31:15	Matthew 2:16-18
He would go to Egypt and come back	Hosea 11:1	Matthew 2:13-15; 19-22
John the Baptist would prepare the way before the Messiah	Isaiah 40:3; Malachi 3:1	Matthew 3:1-3; 11:7-10; 17:10-13; Mark 1:2-4; Luke 1:13-17; 66-79; 3:1-20
Jesus would be the Prophet, like Moses, that God promised to send	Deuteronomy 18:15	John 6:14; Acts 3:18-26
He would do miracles and preach good news to the poor	Isaiah 35:5-6; 58:6; 61:1-2a	Matthew 11:2-6; Luke 4:16-30; 7:14-23
He would speak to the people in parables	Isaiah 6:6-9	Mark 4:1-12
He would ride into Jerusalem on a donkey	Zechariah 9:9	Matthew 21:1-5
He would be rejected by His people	Isaiah 53:3	Luke 23:13-18; John 1:10-13
He would be betrayed by a friend	Psalm 42:9	Matthew 26:14-16; 26:47-56; Mark 14:10
He would be sold for 30 pieces of money	Zechariah 11:12-13	Matthew 26:14-15; 27:3-10
He would be abandoned by His followers	Zechariah 13:7	Matthew 26:31, 55-56
He is the Christ-He will sit at the right hand of God, and will return on the clouds of heaven	Matthew 26:63-64 (see also Psalm 110:1 and Daniel 7:13)	Future
He would be forsaken by God	Psalm 22:1	Matthew 27:45-46; Mark 15:34
His hands and feet would be pierced	Psalm 22:16	Luke 24:37-39; John 20:27
People would divide up His clothes	Psalm 22:18	Matthew 27:35; John 19:24
None of His bones would be broken	Psalm 34:20	John 19:33-37
He would be the rejected cornerstone	Psalm 118:22-23	Acts 4:8-12
People would cry out to Jesus the Messiah as He entered Jerusalem	Psalm 118:25-26	Matthew 21:6-11
He would be a sacrifice for our sin	Isaiah 53:6, 12	Romans 5:6, 8; 1 Corinthians 15:3
He would die with criminals	Isaiah 53:12	Matthew 27:38; Mark 15:27; Luke 23:33
He would be buried in a rich man's grave	Isaiah 53:9	Matthew 27:57-60; Mark 15:42-26
God would raise Him from the dead	Psalm 16:8-11; Matthew 17:9; 20:19; Mark 8:31; 9:31	Matthew 29:1-9; Mark 16:1-13; Luke 24:1-8; Acts 2:29-32; 1 Corinthians 15:4-8
He would cast out demons and heal people from their illnesses		Luke 4:31-41
He would preach good news of the kingdom of God		Luke 4:42-44

Notes

1. John Forster, *The Life of Charles Dickens* (London: Chapman and Hall, 1901), 906.

2. Johann Wolfgang von Goethe, quoted in Adolph Saphir, *The Divine Unity of Scripture* (London: Hodder and Stoughton, 1892), 15.

3. Horace Greeley, quoted in William Wallace Everts, *The Christian Apostolate Its Principles Methods & Promise in Evangelism* (Chicago: Revell, 1890), 392.

4. William Wirt, *Sketches of the Life and Character of P. Henry* (Philadelphia: Thomas, Cowperthwaite, 1845), 418.

5. Patrick Henry, quoted in "Patrick Henry's Legacy," *Upper Room Bulletin* 3, no. 15 (February 3, 1917): 171.

6. Charles Hodge, quoted in Josiah Hotchkiss Gilbert, *Dictionary of Burning Words of Brilliant Writers: A Cyclopædia of Quotations from the Literature of All Ages* (New York: W. B. Ketcham, 1895), 35.

7. *Public Papers of the Presidents of the United States: Herbert Hoover, 1929* (1974), 136.

8. James E. Jennings, quoted in Charles R. Gerber, *Healing for a Bitter Heart* (Joplin, MO: College Press, 1996), 106.

9. Abraham Lincoln, Reply to Loyal Colored People of Baltimore upon Presentation of a Bible, September 7, 1864, in *Collected Works of Abraham Lincoln*, vol. 7., https://quod.lib.umich.edu/l/lincoln/lincoln7/1:1184?rgn=div1;view=fulltext.

10. Dwight Lyman Moody, *Notes from My Bible: From Genesis to Revelation* (New York: Fleming H. Revell, 1895), 8.

11. See Herbert Spencer, *First Principles: : A System of Synthetic Philosophy* (New York: D. Appleton, 1898), pt. 2, chap. 3, "Space, Time, Matter, Motion, and Force"; and Soylent Communications, "Herbert Spencer," NNDB: Tracking the Entire World, 2011, http://www.nndb.com/people/013/000094728/.

12. "Grand Chief, Sir Michael T. Somare, GCL GCMG CH CF KStJ, Prime Minister of Papua New Guinea: Statement at the World Leaders Forum, Columbia University, New York," September 21, 2006, https://web.archive.org/web/20080318055843/http://www.pm.gov.pg/pmsoffice/PMsoffice.nsf/pages/D4837E336A7B8BD44A2571F90019BE4E?OpenDocument.

ADDITIONAL RESOURCES

13. "The World's 20 Oldest Cities," *Telegraph* (UK), May 30, 2017, https://www.telegraph.co.uk/travel/galleries/The-worlds-20-oldest-cities/1old-jericho/.

14. J. Sidlow Baxter, *Baxter's Explore the Book* (Grand Rapids: Zondervan, 2010), lesson 24.

15. Matthew Henry, "Introduction to Esther: An Exposition, With Practical Observations, of The Book of Esther," Blue Letter Bible, https://www.blueletterbible.org/Comm/mhc/Est/Est_000.cfm.

16. Alfred Lord Tennyson, quoted in art. 7, "A New Interpretation of the Book of Job," *Methodist Review* 95 (May 1913): 419.

17. Martin Luther, quoted in *A Religious Encyclopaedia: Or Dictionary of Biblical, Historical, Doctrinal, and Practical Theology*, ed. Philip Schaff, Samuel Macauley Jackson, and David Schley Schaff (New York: Funk & Wagnalls, 1891), 1186.

18. Thomas Carlyle, On Heroes, Hero-worship and the Heroic in History (London: Chapman & Hall, 1888), 45.

19. Philip Schaff, "General Introduction to the Poetical Books," in *A Commentary on the Holy Scriptures: Critical, Doctrinal, and Homiletical*, ed. Johann Peter Lange and Philip Schaff, vol. 8 (New York: Scribner, 1874): xxxii.

20. Baxter, *Baxter's Explore the Book*, lesson 57.

21. James Martin Gray, *Primers of the Faith* (New York: Revell, 1906), 86.

22. Jack Zavada, "Introduction to the Book of Ezekiel," Thought.Co, updated August 7, 2018, https://www.thoughtco.com/introduction-to-the-book-of-ezekiel-701131.

23. *Expositor's Dictionary of Texts*, "Habakkuk 2: The Free-thinker Among the Prophets," commentary on Habakkuk 2:1, https://biblehub.com/commentaries/edt/habakkuk/2.htm.

Other Books by Tom Doyle

Tom is a master storyteller with several books highlighting God's miraculous work among the Muslim people. His best-known books include *Dreams and Visions* (2012), *Killing Christians* (2015), and *Standing in the Fire* (2017).

Standing in the Fire: Courageous Christians Living in Frightening Times
Not Even ISIS Can Scare Them Off
Followers of Christ need to relearn what it means to stand courageously for thier faith rather than merely survive in a climate of fear. Instead of motivating believers to action, today's headlines appear to be paralyzing them. *Standing in the Fire* demonstrates the church triumphant through the lives of people who stood strong and didn't run away in the face of overwhelming danger. These Middle Eastern heroes of faith fear God more than the terrorist groups like ISIS. Supported by Tom Doyle's commentary on events, the stories included show how these Christians are not living as victims, but victors in Christ.

Killing Christians: Living the Faith Where It's Not Safe to Believe
Could you retain your faith even if it meant losing your life? Your family's lives? To many Christians in the Middle East today, a "momentary, light affliction" means enduring only torture instead of martyrdom. The depth of oppression Jesus followers suffer is unimaginable to most Western Christians. Yet, it is an everyday reality for those who choose faith over survival in Syria, Iran, Egypt, Lebanon, and other countries hostile to the Gospel of Christ. In *Killing Christians*, Tom Doyle takes readers to the secret meetings, the torture rooms, the grim prisons, and even the executions that are the "calling" of countless Muslims-turned-Christians.

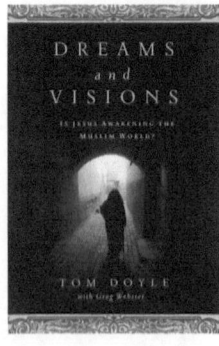

Dreams and Visions: Is Jesus Awakening the Muslim World?
What would you do if Jesus appeared to you in a dream?
What if He came to you in a vision and told you to follow Him? What if these visions continued for over thirty days? Would you believe? Would you put your trust in Him? Would you devote your life to Him? Would you if you were Muslim? *Dreams and Visions* is a remarkable collection of stories directly from the world of Islam. Doyle not only relates these stories, but also addresses the questions: Why would God use dreams to reach the Muslim world? Can dreams be trusted? What happens after these dreams of visions occur?

UNCHARTED MINISTRIES

Did you know there is Good News from the Middle East? Uncharted Ministries seeks:

To inspire the Body of Christ to rise up and join the new great awakening among Jews and Muslims in the Middle East and in uncharted territories around the world.

Want to know more? Check out *unchartedministries.com*

Be amazed at how God wants to use you!

Every Soul Matters,

The Uncharted Ministry Team

www.ingramcontent.com/pod-product-compliance
Lightning Source LLC
LaVergne TN
LVHW041810060526
838201LV00046B/1207